Praise for *Making Every Maths Lesson Count*

Making Every Maths Lesson Count provides an authoritative take on how current ideas about the learning mind can inform lesson and task design in secondary school mathematics, way beyond anything commercial textbooks offer. The reader can use it to develop an informed and critical stance towards teaching approaches and materials, and also as a guide to designing their own. The range of examples presented is exceptional and stimulating.

**Anne Watson, Professor Emerita of
Mathematics Education, University of Oxford**

I really enjoyed the original *Making Every Lesson Count*, and I always learn something when I am lucky enough to hear Emma McCrea speak, so I was incredibly excited to read this maths-specific instalment in the series.

It did not disappoint. I love its structure, its synthesis of research and practical applications, the ideas woven in from all over the world, the section on the great task designer Malcolm Swan, and the recommendation to check out my podcast (fiver in the post, Emma). Above all, I just love that a book like this exists, as I know it will make me a better teacher.

Craig Barton, maths teacher and author of *How I Wish I'd Taught Maths*

Each generation of maths teachers must rearticulate, in their own vernacular, the essential components of effective maths teaching as they see them. In *Making Every Maths Lesson Count*, an accomplished practitioner draws on current research, on her own experience in the classroom, and on the writings of fellow practitioners to provide sage advice and 52 pedagogical strategies rooted in both theory and practice. The important thing is that readers experiment for themselves, and reflect on their experience as they prepare to develop their practice in the future.

**John Mason, Professor Emeritus of Mathematics Education,
Open University, and Honorary Research Fellow,
Department of Education, University of Oxford**

Emma McCrea's *Making Every Maths Lesson Count* is essential reading for all teachers of mathematics, whether experienced or new. It manages that rare gift of being broad yet succinct, and is a reference piece that you'll find yourself coming back to again and again. While providing a solid overview of the state of play in the teaching of mathematics, it is also a jumping-off point to explore the people and ideas that are shaping its future.

Kris Boulton, Director of Education, Up Learn

Making Every Maths Lesson Count is an excellent handbook to contemporary maths teaching for anyone wanting to become a high-performing practitioner.

Bruno Reddy, former head of maths, King Solomon Academy

With *Making Every Maths Lesson Count* Emma McCrea has managed a nearly impossible task: take a lifetime's worth of good advice on teaching mathematics and distil it into one practical and easy-to-read book. She does a great job of balancing the theoretical aspects of the ideas presented with practical suggestions and examples of those theories put into practice. The ideas of dozens of master teachers are incorporated into this book, leading to a work that is greater than the sum of its parts.

David Wees, maths educator, blogger and education consultant

Making Every Maths Lesson Count is a clear and eloquent introduction to the complicated and nuanced skill of high-quality mathematics teaching. From the urgency of conceptual understanding to the fundamentals of teaching for long-term memory, this book highlights and prioritises the most undeniably important components of teaching and learning in the mathematics classroom.

Ed Southall, Mathematics Teacher Trainer, Huddersfield University

Drawing on evidence from the canon of mathematics education and the more recently acknowledged field of cognitive science, *Making Every Maths Lesson Count* is packed full of practical ideas you could apply immediately, advice to embed over time, and wisdom that will be eminently useful for new and seasoned maths teachers alike. This book should be on every maths department's CPD shelf.

Jemma Sherwood, Head of Mathematics,
Haybridge High School and Sixth Form

Accessible, succinct and easily digestible, *Making Every Maths Lesson Count* neatly summarises the key ideas in maths teaching. It is thoroughly evidence-based and is packed full of suggested tasks and activities. I love the prompts encouraging readers to reflect on their practice and think about how they can try out new approaches in the classroom.

Essential reading for trainee maths teachers, and it will be of great benefit to experienced teachers too.

Jo Morgan, maths teacher and creator of resourceaholic.com

In *Making Every Maths Lesson Count* Emma has expertly drawn together all the approaches and strategies a teacher can use to make their pupils better mathematicians. From old favourites like the use of mini whiteboards to more recent techniques such as "silent modelling", each approach is brilliantly exemplified and illustrated.

Simply put, every teacher of maths, whether they are just starting out or have been teaching for 30 years, will find something of value in *Making Every Maths Lesson Count*. It is the book of a lifetime for anyone involved in teaching mathematics.

Peter Mattock, Director of Mathematics,
Brockington College, and author of *Visible Maths*

Making Every Maths Lesson Count is one of the best maths teaching books I've read. Emma takes you on a journey through the principles that underpin the Making Every lesson Count series and expertly adapts these for use in the maths classroom. In an engaging and highly accessible way, she manages to draw on research and expertise from across all aspects of education – which results in an exceptional balance of practical ideas and theory.

Mel Muldowney, maths teacher (previous joint winner of the *TES* Schools
Awards' Maths Team of the Year award) and blogger at *JustMaths*

Making every
maths
lesson count

Six principles to support
great maths teaching

Emma McCrea

Edited by Shaun Allison and Andy Tharby

Crown House Publishing Limited
www.crownhouse.co.uk

First published by

Crown House Publishing Limited
Crown Buildings, Bancyfelin, Carmarthen, Wales, SA33 5ND, UK
www.crownhouse.co.uk

and

Crown House Publishing Company LLC
PO Box 2223, Williston, VT 05495, USA
www.crownhousepublishing.com

First published 2019. Reprinted 2019, 2020.

British Library Cataloguing-in-Publication Data

A catalogue entry for this book is available from the British Library.

Print ISBN 978-178583332-8
Mobi ISBN 978-178583420-2
ePub ISBN 978-178583421-9
ePDF ISBN 978-178583422-6

LCCN 2019932891

Printed and bound in the UK by
Gomer Press, Llandysul, Ceredigion

Foreword by Dylan Wiliam

There is probably no school subject in which public perceptions of the subject are more at variance with the views of its practitioners than in mathematics. I sometimes think that non-mathematicians imagine that mathematicians spend most of their time doing really long divisions. Many years ago, in a book entitled *Do You Panic About Maths?*, Laurie Buxton, a mathematics inspector for the now defunct Inner London Education Authority, had interviewed a number of intelligent, articulate adults about their feelings about mathematics. He concluded that many, and in particular, those who had not been successful at mathematics in school, saw mathematics as:

1   Fixed, immutable, external, intractable, and uncreative.

2   Abstract and unrelated to reality.

3   A mystique accessible to a few.

4   A collection of rules and facts to be remembered.

5   An affront to common sense in some of the things it asserts.

6   A time-test.

7   An area in which judgements not only on one's intellect but on one's own personal worth will be made.

8   Concerned largely with computation.[1]

This is in stark contrast to the views of mathematicians, who frequently talk about the beauty of the subject, and use words like "elegant" to describe particular solutions to a problem. Buxton offered a different list, which much more closely accords with the views of those who are successful at learning mathematics:

1   Experimental, exploratory and creative.

2   Abstract at times but often related to the most practical of problems.

3   Open to all, but (as with all areas of study) to be penetrated more deeply by some than others.

4   A network of consistent relationships, easily remembered when understood.

5   Always reconcilable with the internal logic of the mind.

6   A contemplative subject requiring constant and undivided attention at times but almost never needing to be done in haste.

7   An area in which judgements on one's ability should carry no more weight than in other studies.

8   About relationships in general.[2]

The result is what Keith Stanovich has described as an educational "Matthew effect" based on the passage in the bible: to those that have, more shall be given and for those who have nothing, what little they have will be taken away.[3] Students who experience success in mathematics spend more and more time doing it, getting better and better, while those who find it more difficult come to believe that maths is not for them.

To break this vicious spiral, we have to make sure that students experience success in mathematics, because – as recent research has shown – in mathematics, success causes motivation at least as much as motivation causes success.[4] There is such a thing as 'talent' in mathematics to be sure – some students find learning mathematics easier than others – but as John Carroll showed over half a century ago, in school studies at least, talent, or 'aptitude', is really nothing more than an indication of how much time an individual will take to learn something.[5] Some students learn things quickly, and others take more time – and this is why opportunity cost is the single most important concept in improving educational achievement and closing achievement gaps. If some lessons are spent on things that are not necessary for the intended learning, then this will probably not have much impact on the achievement of students who find learning mathematics relatively easy. But for those who need more time, it is a disaster, and this is why "making every lesson count" is not just a good idea but a moral imperative. If we don't make every lesson count, then we widen the achievement gap. It is as simple as that.

In this book – the latest addition to the Making Every Lesson Count series – Emma McCrea applies the framework developed by Shaun Allison and Andy Tharby to the teaching of mathematics, and the result is a superb resource for anyone who teaches mathematics at any level. The book is well-written, concise – important when your message is that we should make every lesson count! – thoroughly grounded in the realities of teaching mathematics and authoritative, drawing out clear principles from the latest research on memory, learning and motivation. I could go on, but since opportunity cost is the most important concept in educational improvement, your time would be better spent reading what Emma has written ...

Dylan Wiliam, UCL

Endnotes

1   Laurie Buxton, *Do You Panic About Maths? Coping with Maths Anxiety* (London: Heinemann Educational Books, 1981), p. 115.

2   Buxton, *Do You Panic About Maths?*, p. 116.

3   Keith E. Stanovich, Matthew Effects in Reading: Some Consequences of Individual Differences in the Acquisition of Literacy, *Reading Research Quarterly* 21(4) (1986): 360–407.

4   Gabrielle Garon-Carrier et al., Intrinsic Motivation and Achievement in Mathematics in Elementary School: A Longitudinal Investigation of Their Association, *Child Development* 87(1) (2016): 165–175. doi: 10.1111/cdev.12458

5   John B. Carroll, A Model for School Learning, *Teachers College Record* 64(8) (1963): 723–733.

Acknowledgements

It was the incredibly talented and charismatic author Peps Mccrea who started me on this journey when, in late 2017, he waved this tweet from Shaun Allison under my nose:

Calling all #maths teachers – we are looking for an author to write 'Making Every Maths Lesson Count'. Interested?

What followed has been a remarkable adventure featuring bouts of pride (to hear that I was to be welcomed into the Making Every Lesson Count family), apprehension ("I do numbers, not words"), fear ("I'll never finish this") and excitement (at producing an actual book with my name on it).

I owe a great deal to those who helped along the way, particularly members of the incredible maths education community – a group of immensely talented super-humans who are constantly striving to help their students succeed. I hope I have done you justice.

To those who gave up their valuable time to review the book I thank you for your kind words and support. I am greatly indebted to Anne Watson, David Wees, Dylan Wiliam and Kris Boulton for their thoughtful feedback. Thanks to Dylan Wiliam for penning the thought-provoking foreword that sets the perfect tone for the book – it is a delight and an honour to share pages with such words of wisdom.

On a more personal note, thanks to Peps for getting the ball rolling, paving out time for me to write and offering insightful feedback throughout the process. To Shaun and Andy, and David at Crown House Publishing, for their trust in my ability to build upon the good family name. To all those patient, thoughtful educators who endured conversations with me that began, "So, problem solving …" or, "So, factorising …" Deb Friis and the fabulous maths team at the University of Brighton put up with the brunt of it – thank you for pushing my thinking.

To the early readers, Cath McGrath, Wendy McCrea, Trish Dooley and Laura Mawer, who were kind enough to give me their time and valuable thoughts. To Emma Tuck, who diligently worked through edit after edit with me. To Bev at Crown House Publishing for her careful oversight and patience throughout the process (and for having a wonderful Welsh accent). To Jason Ramasami, the creative force behind the fabulous illustrations. To those who were kind enough to allow me to reproduce their work (I hope I represent it accurately).

To my friends and family – thank you for your patience, particularly when I either bored you with a book update or closed you down because progress was slow and I didn't want to talk about it. Vicky and Lucy of the Friday club – thank you for putting up with my regular absences while I wrote.

Last, but not least, to M&M, who inspire me daily.

Contents

Introduction

Teaching maths is not easy. It can feel like all the cards are stacked against us. We teach a subject that is frequently loathed and publicly jibed. For many, "I was rubbish at maths" is worn as a badge of honour. The lack of choice that students get when learning maths can lead to a lack of buy-in. Yet at the same time it is regarded as one of the two most important subjects at GCSE in terms of accountability measures. These factors (and others) result in 40% of maths teachers leaving the profession within their first six years.[1] This retention crisis leaves our maths departments overstretched and our teachers overworked.

There is no doubt that learning maths and being numerate is important. There is a wealth of evidence about the personal and financial impact of poor numeracy to back this up. The Organisation for Economic Co-operation and Development (OECD) found that "high numeracy is particularly correlated with a higher likelihood of; having higher wages, having good to excellent health and being employed",[2] leading to the OECD's director for education and skills, Andreas Schleicher, to state that "good numeracy is the best protection against unemployment, low wages and poor health".[3]

A study by the Institute for Fiscal Studies calculated that students who are 'good' at maths are able to earn around an extra £2,100 per year,[4] and the government released a paper suggesting that getting five or more good GCSEs, including maths and English, would gain them an additional £100,000 over a lifetime.[5] Yet more than 20% of British adults have serious difficulties with numeracy that interfere with basic daily activities.[6] And the impact goes beyond the individual, with poor adult numeracy reportedly draining the UK economy to the tune of £20 billion per year.[7]

Yet there is a strong case that these reasons for learning maths are immaterial. Instead, we learn because we are human, because we are naturally inquisitive and possess an intrinsic thirst for knowledge. We learn because the more we know, the better able we are to make well-balanced, reasoned decisions. We learn maths because, in the words of the Department for Education, it "is a creative and highly interconnected discipline that has been developed over centuries, providing the solution to some of history's most intriguing problems. It is essential to everyday life, critical to science, technology and engineering, and necessary for financial literacy and most forms of employment. A high-quality mathematics education therefore provides a foundation for understanding the world, the ability to reason mathematically, an appreciation of the beauty and power of mathematics, and a sense of enjoyment and curiosity about the subject."[8]

Our classrooms are incredibly complex places. At any given time, the factors influencing the effectiveness of our teaching and the ability of our students to learn are boundless – and this can lead to us relying on intuition as to what might work best. Yet as Yana Weinstein and Megan Sumeracki, co-founders of the Learning Scientists, point out, our own intuitions as to how we learn and how we should teach are not always correct.[9] This book tries to offer a route through this complexity. It does so by sharing a compendium of teaching strategies that are *evidence informed*; that is to say, the strategies presented draw from educational research and findings from the field of cognitive science.[10] Being evidence informed helps because it gives us a head start. Rather than using trial and error to identify what works in the classroom, which is a bit like trying to find a needle in a haystack, research evidence gives us a good starting point. Professor Daniel Muijs, head of research at Ofsted, goes one step further, suggesting that we need to be evidence informed because it is our moral duty (because it exists), for social justice (to close the gap) and for the credibility of our profession.[11]

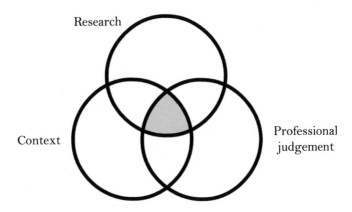

Figure I.1. The sweet spot is at the intersection of research, context and professional judgement

That is not to say that research outcomes will replicate as well, or in the same way, in every classroom. Being evidence informed is one part of the puzzle; adapting to context (type of school, ethos, local demographic, cohort, etc.) and using professional judgement (knowledge of students, values and beliefs) are others. A comparison can be drawn with building a skyscraper: there are principles of physics that need to be respected; principles that if they aren't followed would result in the building falling down. But these principles of physics don't tell you how to build the skyscraper or what it needs to look like.[12] As Dylan Wiliam eloquently said, "Everything works somewhere, and nothing works everywhere."[13]

Having an evidence-informed approach also helps us to avoid jumping on the fad bandwagon. For example, many years ago when I was head of maths, I dutifully 'tested' all the students to identify whether they were visual, auditory or kinaesthetic (VAK) learners and planned lessons accordingly, ensuring that each of these learning styles was catered for. We now know that this teaching strategy is a myth.[14]

The Six Principles

This book utilises the framework developed by Shaun Allison and Andy Tharby in *Making Every Lesson Count*.[15] The framework is comprised of six pedagogical principles that underpin great teaching and learning (see page 5).

The first principle is challenge – "the driving force of teaching".[16] In having high expectations of all our students, regardless of their prior attainment, we can help them to learn more, experience greater success and, most importantly, help them to foster higher expectations of themselves. In Chapter 1 we will also explore why getting students to attend to what it is that we want them to learn is so important.

What follows in the original *Making Every Lesson Count* are two chapters called 'Explanation' and 'Modelling'. This is where it gets a little tricky for us maths teachers. We rarely explain without a model due to the fact that our subject is best conveyed by modelling. Consequently, this book combines explanation and modelling (Chapter 2). We will also consider the role that cognitive load plays in learning and how we can use cognitive load theory to streamline our explanations.

Naturally, practice comes next (Chapter 3), with a focus on how we can use the features of deliberate practice and embed retrieval practice strategies to supercharge the impact of the practice that students do.

We will then investigate how we can use effective questioning (Chapter 4) to either focus student attention or to gain an insight into their thinking. We will take a look at how effective questioning can help us overcome the 'curse of knowledge' and the Dunning–Kruger effect.

Last, but not least, is feedback (Chapter 5), the holy grail of teaching and learning principles. Just as the captain of a ship takes constant readings of weather and currents during a voyage, and then adjusts the speed and bearing in response to those readings, feedback allows teachers to do the same. It enables them to steer their students to their learning destination while making adjustments en route, both in the moment during the lesson and over time through changes to subsequent lessons and schemes of work. Without feedback, we are the captain of a ship adrift at sea.

While unpicking feedback, we also consider the implications of the idea that when we measure learning in a lesson we are not actually measuring learning – we are measuring performance. The measure of learning is if a student still knows and understands the content many months later.

Great maths teaching is aligned with all of these principles; however, they do not represent a lesson plan or a tick-list. This book presents them as individual entities, but in reality they are parts of a whole. They sustain each other. Not only do they help you to plan maths lessons and schemes of work, but they also help you to respond with spontaneity to the ever-changing and ever-complex needs of your students within lessons.

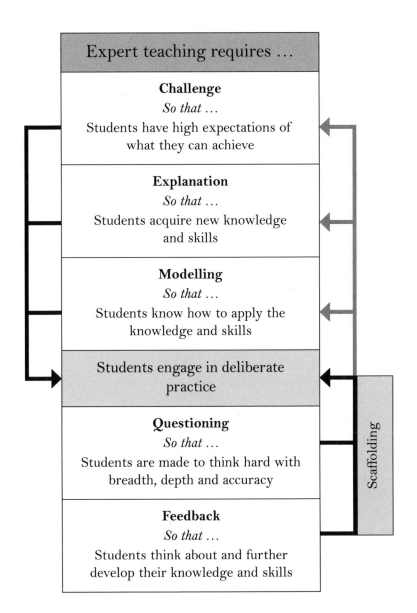

In recent years, the education establishment has lionised the individual lesson. The unrelenting historic emphasis on lesson grading has led to an unhealthy focus on the success of single lessons (or lack thereof). The problem is that learning maths is not speedy, linear or logical. It is slow, erratic and messy, and does not readily conform to hour-long, bite-size chunks. In his book *The Hidden Lives of Learners*, Graham Nuthall brings together findings from various studies to uncover what really goes on in classrooms. One of the most surprising discoveries is that one in three things a student will have learned by the end of a lesson will not be known by any other student, despite our carefully planned and well-intended learning objectives.[17]

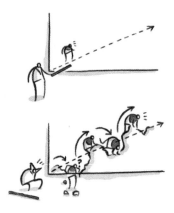

This book and the six principles behind it focus on what goes on in the classroom because that is where we are most able to influence change. Beyond our classrooms, there is a limit to the impact we can have – for example, we are unable to choose what mathematical content we feel is most appropriate for our students because this is mandated through the national curriculum.

The Sutton Trust, a foundation which improves social mobility in the UK through evidence-based programmes, research and policy advocacy, has found that the difference between a 'very effective' teacher and a 'poorly performing' teacher is considerable: "during one year with a very effective maths teacher, pupils gain 40% more in their learning than they would with a poorly performing maths teacher".[18] A different research project found that students in the most effective classrooms learn at four times the speed of those in the least effective classrooms.[19]

In *What Makes Great Teaching?*, Robert Coe and his colleagues from the Sutton Trust identify two features that show strong evidence of impact on student outcomes: pedagogical content knowledge and quality of instruction.[20] These features are within our influence (see Table I.1) and this book has a strong focus on both. However, deep subject knowledge and exceptional instructional design alone are not enough. Alongside these there is a need for excellent classroom management skills and a purposeful effort to foster good relationships based on mutual trust and respect.[21]

Table I.1. What are we able to influence in our teaching?

Within our influence	Partially within our influence	Beyond our influence
Instructional design Subject knowledge Relationships Classroom management Classroom learning climate	Departmental curriculum design Student attitude to maths Student attitude to learning Maths anxiety	Parental influence National curriculum content School learning climate Public attitude to maths Results accountability

One of the difficulties I faced when writing this book was the lack of clarity around the language of learning. For example, the term 'mastery' means different things to different teachers. If we don't have a common understanding of what something means, it can be very difficult to have a meaningful discussion about it. "'When *I* use a word,' Humpty Dumpty said, in rather a scornful tone, 'it means just what I choose it to mean – neither more nor less.'"[22]

To overcome this, I have tried to define exactly what I mean when I use a term. Table I.2 lists the words used throughout the book and their definitions that may otherwise be open to interpretation.

Table I.2. Terms used and their meaning

When I use the word ...	I am using it to mean ...
Example	The models we provide to students to aid their understanding.

When I use the word ...	I am using it to mean ...
Modelling	What we do as teachers to demonstrate a concept or approach (not modelling in the mathematical sense of the word).
Practice	What students do to improve their performance.
Problem	Any task presented to a student.
Problem solving[23]	Solving unfamiliar problems.
Question	A matter which we ask students to focus their attention on or use to elicit information from them.
Teaching	Our classroom practice – that is, what we as teachers do to help students learn.

We also need a shared understanding of what learning maths means. The American National Mathematics Advisory Panel suggests that learning maths requires three types of knowledge: factual, procedural and conceptual.[24] By *factual*, we mean retrieving from memory rather than calculating. For example, if I asked you to calculate 7×8 you would know the solution instantaneously because your response is automated. *Procedural* knowledge describes our ability to select and execute a procedure to solve a given problem – for example, to multiply 38 by 57 we might use the grid or column method. *Conceptual* knowledge, or conceptual understanding as it is more commonly called, relates to how well we understand mathematical concepts and the relationships between concepts. Using the previous example, this would mean having an understanding of what it means to multiply and why the grid or column methods (or even better, both) work.

There is an ongoing chicken and egg debate in maths about whether students should be taught *how* or *why* first. Some argue that if students have a conceptual understanding, they can create their own procedures; this is true for some but not all students. Others argue that conceptual understanding can be developed through procedural knowledge; however, there are students who know that to find the area of a rectangle they need to multiply the length by the width but cannot explain why. The evidence suggests that there is a bidirectional relationship between procedural knowledge and conceptual understanding, therefore they should be taught together wherever possible, so that one will reinforce the other.[25] Unfortunately conceptual understanding is the most difficult to acquire[26] and is developed over time.

It is when our students have secure factual and procedural knowledge *and* deep conceptual understanding that they have the best chance of success. Together, this knowledge enables them to build fluency. By 'fluency' we mean the ability to calculate accurately (find correct solutions), efficiently (using an appropriate strategy or algorithm with speed) and flexibly (adapting strategy and transferring across contexts).[27] It is this fluency that helps students to reason mathematically and solve unfamiliar problems.

We must not underestimate the importance of factual knowledge. As Willingham says, "Data from the last 30 years lead to a conclusion that is not scientifically challengeable: thinking well requires knowing facts … The very processes that teachers value the most – critical thinking processes like reasoning and problem solving – are intimately intertwined with factual knowledge that is in long-term memory."[28]

What is missing from this model is the barrier we face in terms of the attitudes and dispositions our students can sometimes display:

♦ *Poor motivation.* Attempts to motivate students before teaching them new material tend to be unsuccessful. It is better to allow them to experience success and then their motivation and confidence should follow. A good principle for this is that the best way to motivate students is through the content we teach them.

♦ *I'm rubbish at maths* is frequently heard. When a student says they are rubbish at maths, they are attributing their failure to succeed to something that they believe is unchangeable, which, in most cases, is simply not true.

♦ *When am I ever going to use this?* Possibly never, but the more they know about anything, the more they can understand about everything.

♦ *I can't do it.* Add the word *yet* and say: "You can't do it, *yet*. But with hard work and perseverance, you will be able to do it." This uses the language of growth mindset and reinforces the idea that nearly everyone is capable of learning maths.

Good relationships, built on mutual respect and trust, are vital when trying to foster positive attitudes and dispositions. Good relationships stem from having high expectations of students, both in their ability to learn and in their attitude and behaviour for learning, and being clear and consistent in your response when students do not meet these expectations.

Doug Lemov, the author of *Teach Like a Champion*, once quoted a friend as saying, "if you try to catch five rabbits, you catch none".[29] This struck me as a great metaphor for improving our teaching. If we try to add to or develop too many parts of our teaching at once, we are at risk of developing none. We see this in some schools where initiative after initiative is rolled out, never quite leaving enough time to embed the first one before the next one comes along. As you read this book, you will (hopefully) find several ideas that you will want to try in your teaching. Be sure to attempt them one at a time, using the reflective questions at the end of each chapter to support this.

Daniel Willingham asserts that "Teaching, like any complex cognitive skill, must be practiced to be improved."[30] For changes to our teaching to stick, we must make them habits. To form habits, we must practise regularly. Often we forget to do this, so setting ourselves reminders can help. For example, if you wanted to form the habit of going to bed a little earlier every evening to read a book, then setting an alarm on your phone might help until the habit is embedded. In a teaching context, perhaps you want to introduce the use of worked example pairs in your explanations (see Chapter 2). You could add them to your lesson plan pro forma, write a reminder on a sticky note to go on your teacher planner or PC screen or stick a big sign on your desk. Alternatively, tell a colleague about your intentions. We stand a greater chance of success when we share our goals.

Finally, in the words of John Hattie, the author of *Visible Learning*, "know thy impact".[31] We need to be able to measure the impact of the changes we make to our teaching. When I use the word 'measure', I use it loosely. With regard to the example of using worked example pairs during explanations, we could measure impact by reflecting on whether the students are better able to get started on their independent practice without further teacher support. Always try to find a way to assess impact, even if it is a crude measure. Ask yourself, "What change do I expect to see?" As Robert Coe observes, "Whenever we make a change we must try to evaluate its impact as robustly as we can."[32]

In summary, as you read this book, it might be useful to make a list of what you would like to try in your classroom. Select one strategy which you feel will make a powerful change to your teaching, try to work out a way to measure the impact of this change, use reminders to form a habit so that it becomes embedded in your teaching, and then take a moment to

Table I.3. Planning and recording change

Chapter and strategy	When	What can I do to make this a habit?	What change(s) should I see?	How can I measure this change?	Actual observed impact
Explanation and modelling > worked example pairs	Autumn 1	• Adapt lesson plan template to include worked example section • Sticky note on PC • Create worked example pair template slide • Tell Trish about progress weekly	• Students are more successful during independent practice	• Count numbers of students asking for help during practice • Ask students to rate their understanding	
Practice > interleaved practice					
Questioning > probe the thinking	Autumn 2				

enjoy your success before trying something new. Table I.3 offers a suggestion of how you might want to record this process.

Ready? Let's begin with challenge.

Endnotes

1 Rebecca Allen and Sam Sims, *How Do Shortages of Maths Teachers Affect the Within-School Allocation of Maths Teachers to Pupils?* (London: Nuffield Foundation, 2018). Available at: http://www.nuffieldfoundation.org/sites/default/files/files/Within-school%20allocations%20of%20maths%20teachers%20to%20pupils_v_FINAL.pdf.

2 Organisation for Economic Co-operation and Development, Survey of Adult Skills (PIAAC) (2013), cited in All Party Parliamentary Group for Maths and Numeracy. Briefing Paper (2014). Available at: http://www.nationalnumeracy.org.uk/sites/default/files/appg_briefing-paper.pdf, p. 4.

3 Quoted in National Numeracy, Attitudes Towards Maths: Research and Approach Overview (Lewes: National Numeracy, 2015). Available at: https://www.nationalnumeracy.org.uk/sites/default/files/attitudes_towards_maths_-_updated_branding.pdf, p. 2.

4 Claire Crawford and Jonathan Cribb, *Reading and Maths Skills at Age 10 and Earnings in Later Life: A Brief Analysis Using the British Cohort Study*. Research Report REP03 (London: Centre for Analysis of Youth Transitions, 2013). Available at: https://www.ifs.org.uk/caytpubs/CAYTreport03.pdf.

5 Hugh Hayward, Emily Hunt and Anthony Lord, *The Economic Value of Key Intermediate Qualifications: Estimating the Returns and Lifetime Productivity Gains to GCSEs, A Levels and Apprenticeships*. Research Report (London: Department for Education, 2014).

6 Ann Dowker, Intervention for Children with Mathematical Difficulties, *Better: Evidence-Based Education – Mathematics* 6(1) (2014): 10–11 at 10. Available at: http://www.betterevidence.org/issue-14/.

7 Pro Bono Economics, *Pro Bono Economics Report for National Numeracy: Cost of Outcomes Associated with Low Levels of Adult Numeracy in the UK* (March 2014). Available at: https://www.probonoeconomics.com/sites/default/files/files/PBE%20National%20Numeracy%20costs%20report%2011Mar.pdf.

8 Department for Education, National Curriculum in England: Mathematics Programmes of Study. Statutory Guidance (July 2014). Available at: https://www.gov.uk/government/publications/national-curriculum-in-england-mathematics-programmes-of-study/national-curriculum-in-england-mathematics-programmes-of-study.

9 Yana Weinstein and Megan Sumeracki, *Understanding How We Learn: A Visual Guide* (Abingdon and New York: Routledge, 2019).

10 Cognitive science can be described as the study of thought, learning and mental organisation.

11 Daniel Muijs, Making Evidence Count for the Busy Teacher. Presentation at researchEd, Durrington High School, Worthing, 28 April 2018.

12 Adapted from Tom Bennett's interview with Professor Daniel Willingham in *researchED* 1(1) (2018): 5–8 at 6. Available at: https://researched.org.uk/wp-content/uploads/delightful-downloads/2018/07/researchEDMagazine-June2018.pdf.

13 Dylan Wiliam, Why Teaching Will Never Be a Research-Based Profession and Why That's a Good Thing. Presentation at researchED, Harris Academy, London, 8 September 2014.

14 See http://www.danielwillingham.com/learning-styles-faq.html.

15 Shaun Allison and Andy Tharby, *Making Every Lesson Count: Six Principles to Support Great Teaching and Learning* (Carmarthen: Crown House Publishing, 2015).

16 Allison and Tharby, *Making Every Lesson Count*, p. 7.

17 Graham Nuthall, *The Hidden Lives of Learners* (Wellington: New Zealand Council for Educational Research, 2007).

18 Sutton Trust, *Improving the Impact of Teachers on Pupil Achievement in the UK: Interim Findings* (September 2011). Available at: https://www.suttontrust.com/wp-content/uploads/2011/09/2teachers-impact-report-final.pdf, p. 2.

19 See Eric Hanushek, What If There Are No 'Best Practices'? *Scottish Journal of Political Economy* 51(2) (2004): 156–172, cited in Dylan Wiliam, Content *Then* Process: Teacher Learning Communities in the Service of Formative Assessment. In Douglas B. Reeves (ed.), *Ahead of the Curve: The Power of Assessment to Transform Teaching and Learning* (Bloomington, IN: Solution Tree Press, 2007), pp. 183–206.

20 Robert Coe, Cesare Aloisi, Steve Higgins and Lee Elliot Major, *What Makes Great Teaching? Review of the Underpinning Research* (October) (London: Sutton Trust, 2014). Available at: https://www.suttontrust.com/wp-content/uploads/2014/10/What-Makes-Great-Teaching-REPORT.pdf.

21 The go-to work on classroom management and relationships is Doug Lemov's *Teach Like a Champion 2.0: 62 Techniques That Put Students on the Path to College* (San Francisco, CA: Jossey-Bass, 2015).

22 Lewis Carroll, *Through the Looking Glass* (London: Penguin, 1994 [1872]), p. 100.

23 We examine problem solving further in Chapters 1 and 3.

24 See Daniel T. Willingham, Is It True That Some People Just Can't Do Math?, *American Educator* (Winter 2009–2010): 14–19, 39 at 16. Available at: https://www.aft.org/sites/default/files/periodicals/willingham.pdf.

25 Bethany Rittle-Johnson, Michael Schneider and Jon R. Star, Not a One-Way Street: Bidirectional Relations Between Procedural and Conceptual Knowledge of Mathematics, *Educational Psychology Review* 27(4) (2015): 587–597. DOI: 10.1007/s10648-015-9302-x

26 See Willingham, Is It True That Some People Just Can't Do Math?

27 Jennifer M. Bay-William and Amy Stokes-Levine, The Role of Concepts and Procedures in Developing Fluency. In Denise Spangler and Jeffrey J. Wanko (eds), *Enhancing Professional Practice with Research Behind Principles to Action* (Reston: VA: NCTM, 2017), pp. 61–72.

28 Daniel T. Willingham, Why Don't Students Like School? Because the Mind Is Not Designed for Thinking, *American Educator* (Spring 2009): 4–13 at 8. Available at: https://www.aft.org/sites/default/files/periodicals/WILLINGHAM%282%29.pdf.

29 See Craig Barton, Doug Lemov: Teach Like a Champion and Top Tips for Delivering Training, *Mr Barton Maths Podcast* [audio] (13 November 2017). Available at: http://www.mrbartonmaths.com/blog/doug-lemov-teach-like-a-champion-and-top-tips-for-delivering-training/.

30 Willingham, *Why Don't Students Like School?*, p. 147.

31 John Hattie, Know Thy Impact, *Educational Leadership* 70(1) (2012): 18–23.

32 Robert Coe, Improving Education: A Triumph of Hope Over Experience. Inaugural lecture, Durham University, 18 June 2013. Available at: http://www.cem.org/attachments/publications/ImprovingEducation2013.pdf, p. xvi.

Chapter 1
Challenge

Daniel Willingham, a professor focusing on the application of cognitive psychology to education, lays out the facts for us: "While it is true that some people are better at math than others – just like some are better than others at writing or building cabinets or anything else – it is also true that the vast majority of people are fully capable of learning [school] mathematics."[1] It is simply not true, in the majority of cases, that students can't do maths.

However, it is clear that in order to be successful, some students require greater levels of perseverance and hard work. For these individuals, and in fact all students, we need to ensure that we are challenging them by having high expectations of both the level of thinking we expect them to achieve and their attitude to working hard, while also (where necessary) supporting them by scaffolding the challenge.

Before we can consider what this challenge looks like in our classroom, we must first consider what learning might look like. Therein lies a problem. We might, for example, observe that students are busy completing lots of work, and we could infer from this that they are learning. But perhaps these students are busy because the work is too easy for them. Professor Robert Coe suggests that these and other easily observable features are "poor proxies for learning". The problem we have is that learning is *invisible.*

**Poor proxies for learning
(easily observed, but not really about learning)**

1   Students are busy: lots of work is done (especially written work).

2   Students are engaged, interested, motivated.

3   Students are getting attention: feedback, explanations.

4   Classroom is ordered, calm, under control.

5   Curriculum has been 'covered' (i.e. presented to students in some form).

6   (At least some) students have supplied correct answers (whether or not they really understood them or could reproduce them independently.

Figure 1.1. Poor proxies for learning[2]

This leaves us with a rather awkward issue. If these things are not indicative of learning taking place, then what is? A good place to start is to reflect upon what we mean by 'learning'.

Educational psychologists Paul Kirschner and John Sweller define learning as "a change in long-term memory".[3] Long-term memory is where we store everything – our very own Wikipedia, if you like. Daniel Willingham suggests that "memory is the residue of thought".[4] By putting these together, we arrive at this: *learning is a permanent change in long-term memory caused by thinking which happens over time* (Figure 1.2).[5]

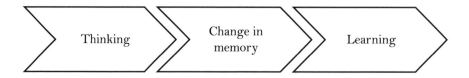

Figure 1.2. Simplified model for learning over time

It is now clear that challenging students to think is crucial. Frustratingly, this is not as straightforward as it sounds. Not only do we need to carefully manage both *what* our students are thinking about and *how hard* they are thinking, but we need to ensure that they are thinking in the first place. Willingham says that "People are naturally curious, but we are not naturally good thinkers; unless the cognitive conditions are right, we will avoid thinking."[6] Hence the importance of focusing student attention.

Students learn what they attend to,[7] meaning that what they learn is greatly influenced by what their attention is focused on. Craig Barton's Swiss roll incident is a great example of the importance of attention. Craig had set his Year 7s an unfamiliar problem to identify the minimum number of cuts needed to share seven Swiss rolls equally between twelve people. Wanting to model the solution, he dutifully purchased said Swiss rolls, rolled up his sleeves and gave his students a memorable 'maths in action' experience. Many years later, a student lamented that maths was boring and not fun like "the Swiss roll lesson". Yet when the student was asked what she thought the lesson was about she replied, "Swiss rolls".[8]

In this scenario, the student's attention was focused on Swiss rolls instead of on the underlying mathematical ideas that were being explored. The student only remembered what she attended to – Swiss rolls. This episode reveals why strategies such as enquiry and discovery learning with minimal guidance can be ineffective. They fail because student attention is not sufficiently attuned to what it is they need to learn. Thus our model for learning becomes that in Figure 1.3.

Figure 1.3. Model for learning over time

Next we need to ask ourselves what happens once attention is suitably focused. This is where working memory, the gatekeeper to long-term memory, comes into play. To enter into long-term memory, information must pass through the working memory, which has a very limited capacity. Overwhelming working memory is referred to as cognitive overload, and occurs when students are made to attend to too many things. They consequently fail to learn anything. The converse is when students fail to learn anything new because the cognitive load is too low. We will examine how to manage cognitive load in Chapter 2.

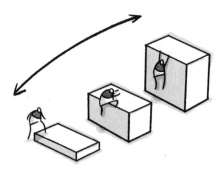

When Cambridge Mathematics pooled the research on working memory, they found that it is particularly important when learning maths. They also found that around a quarter of the differences in mathematics outcomes can be explained by differences in working memory capacity.[9]

As well as challenge being a lever for learning through thinking, challenge also arises when considering the provision for higher prior attainers.[10] For example, in *Mathematics: Made to Measure*, Ofsted found that "More-able pupils in Key Stages 1 to 4 were not consistently challenged."[11] While it is hugely important that we challenge our higher prior attainers, it is equally important to challenge all of our learners.

Before uncovering some strategies for challenge, let's have a recap. We can think of challenge as meaning:

♦ High expectations, not just for the highest prior achievers but for *all* students, all of the time.

♦ *Focusing and regulating* student attention to create optimal conditions for thinking.

Strategies

The first batch of strategies will help us to quantify and ramp up challenge in our teaching. Later on, we will ruminate on the tough stuff, when the strategies will prompt us to challenge ourselves to reflect on the roles that subject knowledge, planning and differentiation play in our ability to challenge students.

Before we jump in, let's take a moment to address one of the thorniest issues in maths education – that of *problem solving*. It is thorny for many reasons, not least because there is no clear consensus of what constitutes a problem. As the Education Endowment Foundation's *Evidence Review* puts it: "At one extreme, any task presented to a student may be defined as 'a problem'. ... At the other extreme, problem solving may be understood to take place only when students are presented with a task for which they have no immediately applicable method, and consequently have to devise and pursue their own approach."[12]

To help clarify this situation so that we have a common understanding of what is meant when we use the term problem solving, I suggest we do two things:

1 Refer to *all* tasks as problems.

2 Define *problem solving* to mean solving *unfamiliar problems*, whereby unfamiliar problems are problems that students possess the requisite knowledge to solve but have not yet met.

What makes this tricky is that familiarity will vary from student to student based on their prior knowledge; thus we cannot say that any given problem is familiar while another is not. More helpful is to think of problems as existing on a spectrum of familiarity with the students positioned at various points along this spectrum, depending on their prior knowledge. Our aim, when we want students to solve problems, is to incrementally nudge them along this spectrum, so that over time they move towards the unfamiliar (see Figure 1.4).

In Figure 1.4, student A is positioned such that they are familiar with the concept of area and have mastered how to find the area of circles and squares. They have not yet met the problems shown above their position on the spectrum, but they do possess the knowledge needed to solve them.

It is worth noting here that asking a student to differentiate x^2, when they have never been taught differentiation, is not an unfamiliar problem; it is an *inaccessible* problem since they lack the requisite knowledge. Likewise, in Figure 1.4, student B has not yet been taught how to find the area of a circle; thus, all of the problems that require an understanding of how to find the area of a circle are inaccessible for them until they acquire and master this knowledge. If we want our students to solve problems successfully, we must make sure they have mastered the necessary knowledge.

Note that when we expose our students to an unfamiliar problem, it ceases to be unfamiliar – it becomes familiar. The more we do this over time, the more we add to a student's catalogue of familiar problems, which, in turn, supports them to reach further unfamiliar problems.

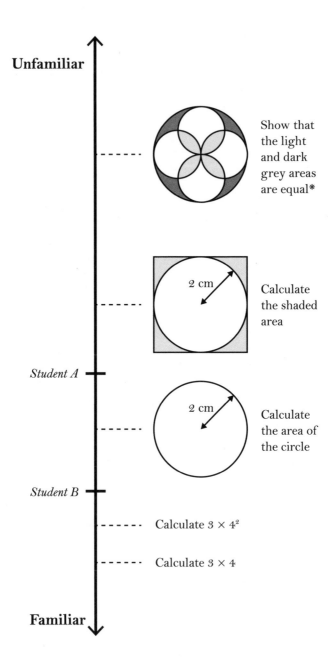

Figure 1.4. Problems on a familiarity spectrum

* This problem was created by John Mason.[13]

Consequently we have three groups of problems:

1   Familiar problems: the student has the requisite knowledge and has met the problem before.

2   Unfamiliar problems: the student has the requisite knowledge and has not yet met the problem before.

3   Inaccessible problems: the student does not yet have the requisite knowledge.

1. Quantify and Ramp Up Challenge

If we want to ensure that we challenge our students with different types of problems, it would be useful to be able to quantify the level of challenge in the problems we use in the classroom. Once we have gauged the level, we can use this understanding to leverage challenge. Two strategies are valuable to us here: Depth of Knowledge levels and the FICT framework. We will examine each of these in turn.

Depth of Knowledge (DoK)

First off, have a quick go at the two problems in Figure 1.5 and consider the level of challenge presented by each.

Add the two numbers below to find the sum	Using the digits 1–9 (no more than once each), fill in the boxes to make the largest sum
$45 + 23$	$\square\square + \square\square$

Figure 1.5. Two problems with differing levels of challenge[14]

The problem on the left presents minimal challenge and requires limited thought. The one on the right offers greater challenge by compelling students to think hard. Yet they are both valid problems to ask, depending on the student's prior knowledge of adding two-digit numbers.

What would be useful to us is if we could somehow quantify these differing levels of challenge so that we are better able to monitor the challenge we afford our students. This is where the Depth of Knowledge (DoK) framework comes into play. Originally developed by American researcher Norman Webb, DoK helps us to describe and classify the level of challenge in problems. The framework consists of four levels (with level 1 being low and level 4 high).[15] Using the descriptors in Table 1.1, can you identify the DoK level of the two problems in Figure 1.5?[16]

Table 1.1. DoK level descriptors[17]

Level 1	*Recall* This level involves the recall of information (fact, definition, term or property), the use of a procedure, or applying an algorithm or formula. It also includes one-step word problems.
Level 2	*Skills and concepts* The skills and concepts level involves demonstrating conceptual understanding through models and explanations, comparing and classifying information, and estimating and interpreting data from a simple graph. At level 2, students would be expected to make some decisions, such as how to approach the problem.
Level 3	*Strategic thinking* This level of complexity involves reasoning, planning and using evidence to solve a problem or algorithm. At level 3, students would be expected to make and test conjectures, interpret information from a complex graph, solve complex problems, explain concepts, use concepts to solve non-routine problems and provide mathematical justifications when more than one response or approach is possible.
Level 4	*Extended thinking* Level 4 tasks require the most complex cognitive effort. Extended thinking requires complex reasoning, planning and thinking generally over extended periods of time (but not time spent only on repetitive tasks). At level 4, students may be asked to relate concepts to other content areas or to real-world applications in new situations.

Robert Kaplinsky, a maths teacher in the United States, has explored the use of DoK levels to quantify and monitor challenge in his teaching. In Figure 1.6, we can see his examples of what problems might look like for each of the three levels across different topics. Note that level 4 tasks tend to be undertaken over an extended period of time, hence their omission.[18]

	DoK 1	DoK 2	DoK 3
Indices	Evaluate 3^4	Using the digits 1–9 (no more than once each), fill in the boxes to make two true equations. $\square^{\square} = 64$ $\square^{\square} = 64$	Using the digits 1–9 (no more than once each), fill in the boxes to make the greatest value possible. $\square^{\square} = \square\square\square$
Fractions on a number line	Which letter represents $\frac{7}{12}$?	Label the point where $\frac{3}{4}$ belongs on the number line. Be as precise as possible.	Create five fractions using the digits 0–9 exactly once each and place them on a number line.
Solving equations with unknowns on both sides	Solve $3x + 2 = -2x + 4$	Using the digits 1–9 (no more than twice each), fill in the boxes to make an equation with no solutions. $\square x + \square = \square x + \square$	Using the digits 1–9 (no more than once each), fill in the boxes to make an equation with a solution that is closest to zero. $\square x + \square = \square x + \square$

	DoK 1	DoK 2	DoK 3
Area and perimeter	Find the perimeter of a rectangle that measures 4 units by 8 units.	List the measurements of three different rectangles that each have a perimeter of 20 units.	What is the greatest area you can make with a rectangle that has a perimeter of 24 units?

Figure 1.6. Examples of DoK levels 1–3 for various topics[19]

Now try it out. Take a look at the practice you have planned for the students to complete in your next lesson and use DoK levels to quantify the level of challenge. Note that it is important for the students to engage in practice at all levels on a regular basis (except level 4 which will happen far less frequently). Level 1 problems are a necessary scaffold for the procedural knowledge that will enable students to access higher level problems. Kaplinsky suggests starting with level 1 and moving on to higher levels when the students are ready. Finally, it is important to remember that increasing the DoK level is not about the task taking longer (except in the case of level 4) or the mathematical content necessarily being more difficult. Higher DoK levels require more thought, which, as Coe suggests, may be indicative of learning.

Now that we have a sense of how to quantify challenge using DoK, we can use the framework to help us ramp up the challenge. Have a go: start with a level 1 problem (generally a one-step procedural problem) and create a level 2 and 3 version using the descriptors in Table 1.1 and the examples in Figure 1.6 as guides.

Dan Meyer, a teacher from the United States who advocates for better maths instruction, introduced the idea of 'open middle problems' as being well suited to level 2 and 3 DoK problems. He describes open middle problems as having a 'closed beginning' (meaning they all start with the same initial problem), a 'closed end' (meaning they all end with the same solution) and an 'open middle' (meaning there are multiple ways to approach and ultimately solve the problem).[20] A closed end avoids the difficult issue sometimes encountered with open tasks whereby students take different journeys, reach different findings and are focused on different aspects. Open middle problems often have multiple ways of solving them, may involve optimisation so that it is easy to get a solution but more challenging to get the best or optimal solution, and may appear to be simple and procedural in nature but turn out to be more challenging and complex when you start to solve them. Examples of open middle problems are shown in Figure 1.7.

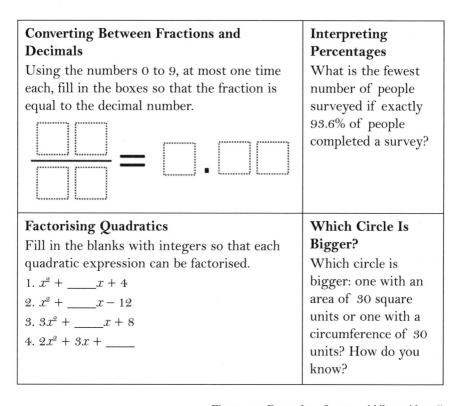

Converting Between Fractions and Decimals	**Interpreting Percentages**
Using the numbers 0 to 9, at most one time each, fill in the boxes so that the fraction is equal to the decimal number.	What is the fewest number of people surveyed if exactly 93.6% of people completed a survey?
Factorising Quadratics Fill in the blanks with integers so that each quadratic expression can be factorised. 1. $x^2 +$ ____ $x + 4$ 2. $x^2 +$ ____ $x - 12$ 3. $3x^2 +$ ____ $x + 8$ 4. $2x^2 + 3x +$ ____	**Which Circle Is Bigger?** Which circle is bigger: one with an area of 30 square units or one with a circumference of 30 units? How do you know?

Figure 1.7. Examples of open middle problems[21]

These and other problems can be found at www.openmiddle.com and are searchable by DoK level and/or topic.

FICT Framework

An alternative way to quantify challenge is by using the FICT framework. It uses four factors to categorise a task's level of challenge: familiarity[22], independence, complexity and technical demand.[23] In maths this means:

♦ *Familiarity* – whether a student has previously been exposed to a similar problem.

♦ *Independence* – the level of autonomy students experience.

♦ *Complexity* – how accessible the problem is.

♦ *Technical demand* – how difficult the mathematics is.

If we consider each of these factors to be on a variable scale, we can adjust them to increase (or decrease) the level of challenge of a problem. Our goal, in terms of challenge, is for students to succeed with solving problems that have low familiarity (i.e. are unfamiliar) and high levels of independence, complexity and technical demand.

Table 1.2. Low and high familiarity, independence, complexity and technical demand

	Low	**High**
Familiarity	Unfamiliar problems – those that students have the knowledge to solve but have not yet met.	Minimally different problems, e.g. $2x + 5 = 7$ and $2x + 6 = 8$
Independence	Students rely heavily on teacher input and peer support during the lesson, which has a single focus.	Problems are solved without support (teacher, peers, worked examples, etc.) alongside unrelated problems (interleaved[24]).
Complexity	The steps required to solve the problem are obvious and/or there is a single solution.	It is not immediately obvious how to solve the problem and/or there are many possible solutions to the problem.
Technical demand	The problem is mathematically easy.	The mathematics involved is difficult.

A FICTometer (Figure 1.8) helps to model this process. It works like an old graphic equaliser (I've also heard it called a graFICT equaliser – an equally terrible name).

For example, let's say the students are working in pairs, practising adding fractions by calculating the solutions to problems similar to $\frac{2}{5} + \frac{1}{10}$, having just been taught how to do so by their teacher. This problem is high in familiarity and low on independence and complexity. The technical demand is not low, given that the denominators are different, but perhaps not medium since one of the denominators is a factor of the other. These ratings are represented in Figure 1.8.

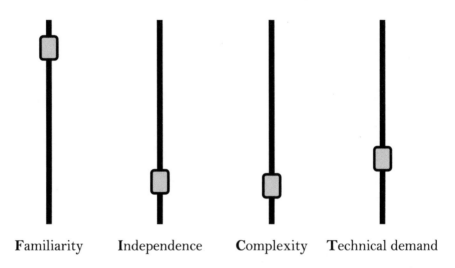

Familiarity   Independence   Complexity   Technical demand

Figure 1.8. The FICTometer/graFICT equaliser tool
displaying ratings for the problem $\frac{2}{5} + \frac{1}{10}$

We can vary each of the features to remove scaffolding and increase the level of challenge. Here are some examples:

♦ Decrease the *familiarity* by asking the students to calculate $\frac{2}{5} + \frac{1}{10} + \frac{2}{5}$ or $\frac{2}{5} + \frac{?}{?} = \frac{1}{2}$ or the perimeter of a rectangle whose side lengths are fractions.

♦ Increase *independence* by asking students to work independently, by setting similar problems to do as homework or by asking them to tackle a similar problem months later.

♦ Increase *complexity* by asking the students to find two different fractions that add to give $\frac{1}{2}$ or set the task in Figure 1.9.

♦ Increase the *technical demand* by including mixed numbers (medium) or surds (high).

$$\frac{1}{6} \quad \frac{1}{25} \quad \frac{3}{5} \quad \frac{3}{20} \quad \frac{4}{15} \quad \frac{5}{8}$$

Add together as many of the six fractions as you like to get an answer that is as near to 1 as possible. You can use each fraction only once.

Figure 1.9. Increasing complexity[25]

Beyond using DoK levels, open middle problems and the FICT framework, there are some other practical ways to ramp up challenge that are worth exploring:

♦ Creating opportunities for students to practise reasoning by explaining their thinking both verbally and in writing.

♦ Using goal-free problems (see Chapter 3).

♦ Getting students to generalise (see Table 1.3).

Table 1.3. Generalising examples

Topic	Examples	
Adding fractions	$\frac{a}{b} + \frac{c}{b} =$	$\frac{a}{b} + \frac{c}{d} =$
Expanding brackets	$(a + b)(c + d) =$	$(a + b)^2 =$
Mean	What is the mean of a, b and c?	Write an expression for the mean of any two consecutive numbers
Volume	A cylinder has radius a cm and height b cm. What is its volume?	A cylinder has radius r cm and height h cm. What is its volume?

2. Build Resilience

One of the greatest issues we face when challenging our students is their lack of resilience. Many young people, understandably, are loath to keep trying when they feel success is beyond their reach. Often they attribute this lack of success to a lack of ability, rather than a lack of resilience (assuming that the problem they have been asked to tackle is, in fact, within their reach).

This struggle is important to the process of learning. Professors Elizabeth and Robert Bjork, researchers specialising in the science of learning, suggest that struggle is what makes learning stick.[26] The issue for us as teachers is to get the balance right. Too much struggle and students lose motivation; too little and the benefits of the struggle are lost. Unfortunately, this balance is hard to strike – the perfect level of struggle varies from student to student based on their prior knowledge and confidence.

One strategy to build resilience is to change the focus. Instead of concentrating on the final solution, reward the journey. When students are faced with a multi-step problem or one that has many solutions, award marks for each correct step or iteration they complete. For example, if tasking students with, "What is the greatest area you can make with a rectangle that has a perimeter of 24 units?" award marks for each correct attempt.

Open Middle has an excellent template for this, which not only awards students a mark out of two for each attempt, but encourages reasoning by offering them an additional two marks for their explanation.[27] Plus, due to the template having space for six iterations, it sets the expectation that problems may take six or more attempts to resolve.

3. Scaffold the Challenge

When a challenge lacks scaffolding, students can lose motivation and confidence. Getting the scaffold right is tough; there should be lots at the start of a learning episode, which is slowly removed as the students' competency improves. It is similar to when babies learn to walk. At first they use scaffolds – they cruise along sofas, use baby walkers and adults to support them as they take their first steps. With practice, they become more adept, taking a few steps at a time without help. Eventually, after much practice, they can walk without support and they no longer need any scaffolding.

One way to scaffold the struggle is to use question cards. Give each student, pair or group one card (or more if you think they need them). You can use anything as question cards – I use pieces of A6 card with a question mark printed on each. Question cards permit the students to ask the teacher a question at any time – no questions can be asked without one.

The students tend to hoard their question card, saving it for when they really need it. Consequently, they persevere for longer and collaborate better, as they often choose to ask their peers rather than give up their question card. When they do ask questions, they will think hard about what question to ask so they don't waste their card.

Rather than offering practical strategies for our classrooms, the strategies below help to challenge us in our teaching.

4. Know Thy Subject

The Sutton Trust has found that there is strong evidence of the impact of increased pedagogical content knowledge on student outcomes.[28] Thus, secure subject knowledge is essential, especially since teaching maths is markedly more complex than it seems. Let's consider an example. It involves the classic, pervasive misconception that to add fractions, you add the numerators and add the denominators (e.g. $\frac{9}{10} + \frac{7}{10} = \frac{16}{20}$) – a misconception that we work tirelessly to combat.

However, consider this scenario. A student sits a test comprised of two papers. They get 9 out of 10 in the first paper, written as $\frac{9}{10}$. In the second paper they get $\frac{7}{10}$. What do they get in total? $\frac{16}{20}$! Despite not explicitly writing $\frac{9}{10} + \frac{7}{10} = \frac{16}{20}$, there is a risk that the students will infer this regardless. And while there are other reasons that students hold this misconception, until recently I had never considered this one. Worse still, it's a tricky (but important) issue to address effectively.

This insight led me to understand two things more clearly: why students find maths so difficult and the importance of teachers' subject knowledge.

In fact, we need more than subject knowledge – something beyond merely knowing how to solve equations. What is required is subject knowledge *for teaching* (SKfT) – that is, what you need to know and understand beyond the content subject knowledge to enable you to teach the content more effectively.

My attempts to codify the knowledge required to build secure SKfT and create a framework yielded five elements applicable to a mathematical idea, concept or topic:

1   What is the *curriculum* and *exam context?*

2   What is the *prior knowledge* and where does it *progress* to?

3   Are there *multiple representations* and *methods?*

4   Where might students have *misconceptions?*

5   What questions might *probe understanding?* (For more on this check out 'Probe the Thinking' in Chapter 4.)

This framework is particularly useful when planning a learning episode (unit of work). Figure 1.11 represents an attempt to capture this for manipulating algebraic expressions. There is no doubt that secure SKfT better enables us to challenge our students:

> The most effective teachers have deep knowledge of the subjects they teach, and when teachers' knowledge falls below a certain level it is a significant impediment to students' learning. As well as a strong understanding of the material being taught, teachers must also understand the ways students think about the content, be able to evaluate the thinking behind students' own methods, and identify students' common misconceptions.[29]

In addition, keep up to date with subject-specific journals, websites and research papers, and keep abreast of the latest research findings in your subject area. By far the best way to do this is to join Twitter. Don't feel pressured to tweet: following a group of well-informed educators and dipping in to your feed regularly is enough to keep your knowledge fresh.[30] Set yourself a time limit for browsing – I've lost many an hour on Twitter!

Resolve to read at least three books a year, one every term, that will enhance and add extra texture to your pedagogy and subject understanding. You're

Topic:
ALGEBRAIC NOTATION/
MANIPULATION OF EXPRESSIONS

1 Example exam context:

Tom is investigating the two expressions

$xy + z$ and $x(y + z)$

i He finds that both expressions have the same value when $x=1$, $y=2$ and $z=7$. Show that this is true.

ii Tom says that this means that $x(y + z) = xy + z$. Explain why Tom is wrong.

Curriculum context:

- Translate simple situations or procedures into algebraic expressions or formulae
- Cancellation to simplify calculations and expressions
- Substitute numerical values into formulae and expressions
- Simplify and manipulate algebraic expressions
- Understand and use the concepts and vocabulary of expressions, equations, formulae, identities, inequalities, terms and factors

Progression:

- Solving a linear equation with one unknown
- Changing the subject of the formula
- Solving quadratic equations
- Simultaneous equations
- Forming and solving equations

2 Mathematical progression

Prior knowledge:

- Expanding brackets
- Substitution
- Addition/Subtraction
- Multiplication/Division
- BIDMAS
- Understanding sign change

Learning:

- Manipulation of expressions
- Substitution of negative values (more than 1)
- Algebraic notation ($ab = a \times b$ etc.)

3 Multiple methods and representations

Substituting then solving considering BIDMAS:	Expanding then substituting:	Substituting then using grid method:
If $a=2$, $b=3$ and $c=4$: $ab + c$ OR $a(b + c)$ $= (2 \times 3)$ $= 2(3 + 4)$ $+ 4$ $= 2(7)$ $= 10$ $= 14$ $\hspace{3cm} 10 \neq 14$	If $a=1$, $b=3$ and $c=4$: $a(b + c)$ $= ab + ac$ $= (1 \times 3) + (1 \times 4)$ $= 3 + 4$ $= 7$	If $a=1$, $b=3$ and $c=4$: $a(b + c) = 1(3 + 4)$ $\begin{array}{c c c} & 3 & +4 \\ 1 & \boxed{3 \; +4} & =7 \end{array}$
Number: If $a=2$, $b=3$ and $c=4$: $ab + c = (2 \times 3) + 4$ $\hspace{2cm} = 6 + 4$ $\hspace{2cm} = 10$ $a(b + c) = 2(3 + 4)$ $\hspace{2cm} = 2 \times 7$ $\hspace{2cm} = 14$ $\hspace{3cm} 10 \neq 14$	**Algebra:** $a(b + c) = ab + ac$ $ab + ac \neq ab + c$	**Shape:** $ab + ac \neq ab + c$

4 Misconceptions

- $ab = a + b$
- ab is a two digit number, for example 12 as opposed to 1×2
- $a = 1$ because it's the first letter in the alphabet
- b is larger than a, c is larger than b and a (due to their position in the alphabet)
- Letters can only represent integers
- "a is worth 3 because that's how much it was worth last lesson"
- $6x$ is the same as x^6
- $6n = 6 + n$
- $3m + 6 = 9m$ not recognising that unlike terms cannot be combined.
- If every term represents an object, the number must represent something too. For example $4a + 3b + 2c + 1$ is 4 apples, 3 bananas, 2 carrots and 1 what?
- $10x^2 + 2x = 12x^2$ (combining unlike terms)
- $2(x + 6) = 2x + 6$ (not applying multiplication to all terms within the brackets.
- Different letters can't represent the same number. For example x and y can't both equal 3.

5 Probing questions

- Convince me that $(x + 4)$ is the same as $(4 + x)^2$
- What's the same and what's different about: $ab + c$ and $a(b + c)$?
- Does $a(b + c) = ab + c$ only when $a=1$, $b=3$ and $c=4$? Show me some other values that would work. Show me how you would go about answering this question: $a(b + \frac{a}{c})$ when $a=2$, $b=3$ and $c=7$.
- Sarah says that $6m + 3$ can be simplified to $9m$, explain to me why she is wrong.
- Is the following statement always, sometimes or never true: "The value of a is larger than the value of b".
- How would you go about expanding the following and what's the most important thing to remember: $(x + 3)(x + 2)$ ... How about $(x + 3)(x + 4)(x + 1)$?
- Why does $2x + 3x^2$ not equal $5x^2$? Justify your answer.
- How would you explain to an alien the process of substituting values into an expression?
- How could we check that $a(b + c) = ab + ac$?
- What's the same and what's different about an expression and an equation?

Figure 1.11. Capturing subject knowledge *for teaching* (SKfT)[31]

already getting one under your belt; here are some more recommended reads:

- *How I Wish I'd Taught Maths* by Craig Barton.
- *How to Teach Mathematics for Mastery* by Dr Helen Drury.
- *Questions Pupils Ask* by Colin Foster.
- *Visible Maths* by Peter Mattock.
- *How to Enhance Your Mathematics Subject Knowledge: Number and Algebra for Secondary Teachers* by Jemma Sherwood.
- *Yes, But Why? Teaching for Understanding in Mathematics* by Ed Southall.

Finally, if you haven't discovered them already, take a listen to Craig Barton's podcasts. Over the past few years, Craig has interviewed many eminent thinkers and practitioners in maths education and shared their conversation in podcast form.[32]

5. Focus Their Attention

Drawing on the work of Peps Mccrea, the author of *Memorable Teaching*, this strategy helps to make incorporating challenge in our lessons a habit during the planning process. It is simple to do. When planning your lesson, prompt yourself by asking, "What do I want the students to be thinking about?" Once you are able to answer this question, ensure that you design each phase so the students think about what you want them to think about. For example, you might plan a sequence of questions to draw the students' attention to specific features of a worked example, or you might design a set of problems for the students to practise that focus on one particular feature (more on this in Chapter 3).

To remind yourself to do this, it may be worth explicitly including this prompt on your lesson plan pro forma, printing a large copy of the prompt and sticking it to your desk and/or setting it as the screensaver on your computer. This increases the likelihood that, over time, it will become a habit.

6. Differentiation

Much that is promoted as good differentiation practice is both unmanageable and counterproductive. It is not humanly possible to personalise planning for each and every student, nor, as often suggested, is it possible to create three levels of worksheet for every lesson.

The most common form of differentiation for our higher prior attainers is to accelerate them through the curriculum. By doing this we send the wrong message that maths is about working through content rapidly, and in doing so we perpetuate the knowledge gap between our highest and lowest prior attainers. The national curriculum echoes this stance, stating that "pupils who grasp concepts rapidly should be challenged through being offered rich and sophisticated problems before any acceleration through new content. Those who are not sufficiently fluent with earlier material should consolidate their understanding, including through additional practice, before moving on."[33] Strategy 1 in this chapter (Quantify and Ramp Up Challenge) offers ways to do this, and we will explore further sources for rich and sophisticated problems in Chapter 3.

Often, the best provision for those with lower prior attainment is more time to practise in order to embed their understanding. As a department, explore ways to offer this practice beyond their timetabled lessons.

Getting challenge right is tough; it is more difficult than each of the other principles. Unfortunately there is no magic wand. It sits at the intersection of high expectations (for all), subject knowledge (for teaching) and knowing our students – particularly their prior knowledge (Figure 1.12).

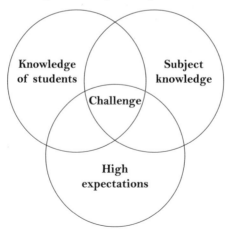

Figure 1.12. The challenge Venn diagram

Reflective questions

♦ Which strategy will have the most powerful impact on your teaching?

♦ Are your students being challenged to think hard? What will the students be thinking about at each phase? How can you get them to think about what you want them to learn?

♦ How do you weave the solving of unfamiliar problems into a learning episode?

♦ What proportions of each of the DoK levels do you typically set your students? Does it change for different classes? Are expectations high for all? How can you further challenge students mathematically?

♦ During a learning episode, are the students exposed to problems that increase in DoK level and/or vary the FICTometer levels?

♦ How do you ensure that your subject knowledge and your subject knowledge for teaching is strong enough to challenge all students?

♦ How do you ensure that you can solve the hardest problems that the students you teach will have to solve?

Endnotes

1   Willingham, Is It True That Some People Just Can't Do Math?, 14.

2   *Source*: Robert Coe, Improving Education: A Triumph of Hope Over Experience. Inaugural lecture, Durham University, 18 June 2013. Available at: http://www.cem.org/attachments/publications/ImprovingEducation2013.pdf, p. xii.

3   Paul A. Kirschner, John Sweller and Richard E. Clark, Why Minimal Guidance During Instruction Does Not Work: An Analysis of the Failure of Constructivist, Discovery, Problem-Based, Experiential, and Inquiry-Based Teaching, *Educational Psychologist* 41(2) (2006): 75–86 at 75.

4   Willingham, *Why Don't Students Like School?*, p. 63.

5   We will explore what we mean by 'over time' in Chapter 5.

6   Willingham, *Why Don't Students Like School?*, p. 3.

7   See Peps Mccrea, *Memorable Teaching: Leveraging Memory to Build Deep and Durable Learning in the Classroom* (n.p.: CreateSpace, 2017).

8   Craig Barton, *How I Wish I'd Taught Maths: Lessons Learned from Research, Conversations with Experts, and 12 Years of Mistakes* (Woodbridge: John Catt Educational, 2018), p. 37.

9   Lucy Rycroft-Smith, Camilla Gilmore and Lucy Cragg, Why Is Working Memory Important for Mathematics Learning?, *Espresso* 10 (2017). Available at: https://www.cambridgemaths.org/Images/429694-traditional-and-progressive.pdf.

10 The terms 'lower prior attainers' and 'higher prior attainers' are preferable to more/less able, higher/lower ability and gifted and talented because these labels can all imply a fixed ability.

11 Ofsted, *Mathematics: Made to Measure* (May 2012). Ref: 110159. Available at: https://assets. publishing.service.gov.uk/government/uploads/system/uploads/attachment_data/file/417446/ Mathematics_made_to_measure.pdf, p. 7.

12 Peter Henderson, Jeremy Hodgen, Colin Foster, Rachel Marks and Margaret Brown, *Improving Mathematics in Key Stages Two and Three: Evidence Review* (London: Education Endowment Foundation, 2018). Available at: https://educationendowmentfoundation.org.uk/public/files/ Support/Links/Campaigns/Maths/EEF_Maths_Evidence_Review.pdf, p. 60.

13 This problem can be seen at Don Steward, Circle Areas, *Median* (30 January 2011). Available at: https://donsteward.blogspot.com/2011/01/circle-areas.html.

14 *Source*: Robert Kaplinsky, Shallowness (Not Depth) of Knowledge, *Robert Kaplinsky* (25 October 2016). Available at: https://robertkaplinsky.com/shallowness-not-depth-knowledge/.

15 An extensive list of these descriptors applied to maths can be found in Marge Petit and Karin Hess, Applying Webb's Depth of Knowledge and NAEP Levels of Complexity in Mathematics (2006). Available at: https://www.nciea.org/sites/default/files/publications/DOKmath_ KH08.pdf.

16 The one on the left is level 1 and the one on the right is level 3.

17 *Source*: Marge Petit and Karin Hess, Applying Webb's Depth of Knowledge and NAEP Levels of Complexity in Mathematics (2006). Available at: https://www.nciea.org/sites/default/files/ publications/DOKmath_KH08.pdf, p. 1.

18 For examples of level 4 problems see https://robertkaplinsky.com/lessons/ and http://www. bowlandmaths.org.uk/.

19 *Source*: Adapted from Robert Kaplinsky, Depth of Knowledge Matrix – Secondary Math, *Robert Kaplinsky* (31 January 2017). Available at: http://robertkaplinsky.com/depth-knowledge-matrix- secondary-math/; and Robert Kaplinsky, Depth of Knowledge Matrix – Elementary & Secondary Math, *Robert Kaplinsky* (4 February 2015). Available at: https://robertkaplinsky.com/ tool-to-distinguish-between-depth-of-knowledge-levels/. Examples suitable for primary can be found in Robert Kaplinsky, Depth of Knowledge Matrix – Elementary Math, *Robert Kaplinsky* (24 January 2017). Available at: https://robertkaplinsky.com/depth-knowledge-matrix- elementary-math/.

20 See http://www.openmiddle.com/whats_open_middle/.

21 *Source*: Robert Kaplinsky and Nanette Johnson via http://www.openmiddle.com.

22 This links to our previous discussion about problem solving.

23 These factors were part of the Functional Skills framework – see https://www.ncetm.org.uk/ resources/14470.

24 Interleaving is explored in Chapter 3.

25 *Source*: Colin Foster, Sum Fractions, *Teach Secondary* 3(5): 48–49. Available at: http://www. foster77.co.uk/Foster,%20Teach%20Secondary,%20Sum%20fractions.pdf.

26 For more on the Bjorks' work applying cognitive psychology to education visit: https://bjorklab. psych.ucla.edu/research/.

27 The template can be found at http://www.openmiddle.com/wp-content/uploads/2016/01/ Open-Middle-Worksheet-v1.2.pdf.

28 Coe et al., *What Makes Great Teaching?*

29 Coe et al., *What Makes Great Teaching?*, p. 2.

30 A curated list of who to follow to get you started can be found at https://twitter.com/ MccreaEmma/lists/who-to-follow and @MccreaEmma.

31 *Source*: Created by Marcus Bennison as part of his subject knowledge enhancement course.

32 See http://mrbartonmaths.com/podcast.

33 See https://www.gov.uk/government/publications/national-curriculum-in-england-mathematics- programmes-of-study/national-curriculum-in-england-mathematics-programmes-of-study.

Chapter 2
Explanation and Modelling

Engelmann holds up a pencil and says, "This is *glerm*." Then he holds up a pen and says, "This is *glerm*." Then he holds up a crayon – also *glerm*. So what is *glerm*? A student responds: "Something you write with." Logical, but wrong … *Glerm* means *up*. The student learned a misrule.[1]

This is an example of how the ambiguity of the examples we share with our students can lead to the wrong conclusion. This is one of the exercises that educationist Siegfried Engelmann uses to teach instructional design. His point is to make us aware of the minefield that teachers must navigate to avoid generating confusion in their students. This is why our explanations must be well planned and coherent.

Maths is full of complex nuances that even teachers of maths are unaware of. Consider this example, courtesy of Dylan Wiliam.[2] We tend to teach students that when no operation is explicitly signposted to infer that the missing operation is multiplication, examples being $4x$, $x(x + 1)$, etc. Using the same principle, consider $4\frac{1}{2}$. It doesn't mean 4 times $\frac{1}{2}$. It means $4 + \frac{1}{2}$. Now consider 41. It doesn't mean 4 times 1.

Another example of this nuance is revealed when finding factors. Listing factors of 8 yields 1, 2, 4, 8. When factorising $\frac{1}{2}x + \frac{1}{2}y$ or $-a - b$ our common factors would be $\frac{1}{2}$ and -1 respectively, yet $\frac{1}{2}$ and -1 are not listed as common factors of 8. How can they exist as factors in one context but seem not to in another? Maths is not as clear cut as we might like to believe. Rules that exist in one context do not always lend themselves to all contexts. This is another reason why our explanations need to be bulletproof, to have perfect clarity and to attend to each and every detail. As Cardinal Thomas Wolsey reputedly said, "Be very, very careful what you put into that head, because you will never, ever get it out."

Explanation is the skill of making abstract, complex concepts clear and concrete in students' minds. Modelling is walking the students through problems and procedures so that we narrate the thought processes they will need to apply. The boundaries between the two are blurred in maths – explaining without modelling would render our subject unintelligible. Explanation and modelling are entwined and occur concurrently. We rarely explain maths without modelling, and the use of models helps us to explain, therefore this chapter considers them together.

What is crucial to our explanations is that they build on prior knowledge: "Prior knowledge determines what students can learn; learning is made easier when new knowledge is connected to existing knowledge."[3] Learning new knowledge is like adding bricks when building a wall. If bricks are missing low down in the wall, the foundations are insecure and the wall will collapse.[4]

As touched on in Chapter 1, one of the main barriers restricting the effectiveness of our explanations is the limited capacity of working memory. To learn, we must transfer information from working memory to long-term memory so that it can be stored and later retrieved. Our working memory is where the local and immediate processing occurs and it has only a small capacity in terms of time and space.[5] If this limited capacity is exceeded, our working memory is overloaded – referred to as cognitive overload. When this happens we are unable to transfer the content of our working memory to long-term memory and no learning occurs.

We can think of working memory and cognitive overload by considering a juggling analogy. It is relatively easy to juggle two or three balls at once, but if we add more and more balls we will likely drop them all. If we were to model how to find the missing angle of a right-angled triangle from start to finish in one go, without having previously taught this in smaller steps (labelling the sides of a triangle, rearranging the trig ratios, etc.), it would likely lead to cognitive overload. The implication is that the understanding of new ideas can be impeded if students are confronted with too much information at once.[6]

In order to accommodate the limitations of working memory, we need to regulate the amount of cognitive work (cognitive load) demanded during explanation and practice. John Sweller's cognitive load theory is about optimising the load on students' working memories to help maximise their learning.[7] To put this theory in perspective, Dylan Wiliam took to Twitter to say, "I've come to the conclusion Sweller's Cognitive Load Theory is the single most important thing for teachers to know."[8] Consequently, we draw on this theory throughout this chapter.

Strategies for Explanation and Modelling

1. Isolate the Skill

One feature of deliberate practice (which we explore more fully in Chapter 3) is to isolate the skill. According to Daisy Christodoulou, "If we want pupils to develop a certain skill, we have to break that skill down into its component parts and help pupils to acquire the underlying mental model."[9] Rather than presenting skills in large complex chunks, which can lead to cognitive overload, we break them down into smaller components, crafted in a carefully chosen order, that accumulate to achieve greater success with a larger, well-defined goal.

A useful analogy can be made with sport. Most professional sports players isolate skills during training. Footballers will practise one-touch passing, tackling or set pieces so that, when playing a full game, they are more likely to be successful.

The most effective way to isolate the skill is to chunk the skill into small concise steps – a process called atomisation (a term first coined by Bruno Reddy and later developed by Kris Boulton[10]). For example, when teaching trigonometry in right-angled triangles, our final goal is for students to be able to solve problems with right-angled triangles using trigonometry, but this goal has a swath of knowledge and skills tied up in its success. Isolating this skill yields the following (inexhaustive) list of steps:

1 To identify a right-angled triangle.

2 To calculate the sine, cosine and tangent of a given angle using a calculator.

3 To calculate the inverse sine, cosine and tangent of a given number using a calculator.

4 To solve equations (including when the unknown is a denominator).

5 To solve equations that contain a trigonometric function.

6 To label the sides of a right-angled triangle using hypotenuse, opposite and adjacent.

7 To recall the trigonometric ratios.

8 To identify which trigonometric ratio to use.

9 To find the length of an unknown side of a right-angled triangle using a trigonometric ratio.

10 To find the size of an unknown angle of a right-angled triangle using a trigonometric ratio.

11 To find the length of unknown sides or unknown angles of a right-angled triangle embedded within 2D shapes.

12 To find the length of unknown sides or unknown angles of a right-angled triangle in word problems.

13 To find the length of unknown sides or unknown angles of a right-angled triangle within a 3D shape.

14 To identify scenarios that require the application of the trigonometric ratios.

15 To be able to solve unfamiliar problems that require the application of the trigonometric ratios.

We do this before teaching a learning episode, so the route to the overarching goal is made explicit. Planning individual lessons becomes much easier and quicker as we can work through the list of steps. They also prompt us to activate any required prior knowledge – for example, the first and fourth steps in our list are likely to be prior knowledge that could be checked during a starter.

The remaining strategies for explanation and modelling tend to fall into one of two distinct categories. The first group of strategies help us to improve coherence and clarity by focusing on show and tell – what we show students and what we say to them to help them better understand. The second group provoke deeper understanding by building a bridge from the concrete to the abstract.

Purpose	Strategies
Show	2 Worked Examples
	3 Concept/Non-concept
Tell	4 Less is More
	5 Silence is Golden
	6 Speak Proper
Bridging concrete to abstract	7 Concrete, Pictorial, Abstract (CPA)
	8 Representations
	9 Dynamic Representations
	10 Gesture
	11 Analogy

Strategies for Show

2. Worked Examples

One of the most effective ways to regulate cognitive load is to use worked examples. A 'worked example' is a problem that has already been solved for the student, with every step fully explained and clearly shown.[11]

Sweller's work within the framework of cognitive load theory tells us that "Studying worked examples provides one of the best, possibly the best, means of learning how to solve problems in a novel domain."[12] This does not seem like news to maths teachers – after all, modelling worked examples at the board is at the very heart of our explanations. What is interesting, however, is the list of specific ways in which it is recommended that we use them.

Worked Example Pairs

For many years, I thought that my approach to explanation was effective. I would model several worked examples (which became increasingly difficult) with the class at the board, narrating and asking questions as I went. Then I would ask the students to practise lots of problems independently, perhaps from a worksheet. Little did I know that this approach of modelling numerous worked examples, followed by practice, has been shown to have the *worst* learning outcomes.[13] In hindsight, this makes sense. Attending to many different examples and remembering the subtle nuances of each of one until the time comes to practise them is difficult; in fact, it is likely to lead to cognitive overload.

A more effective approach is to use worked examples in pairs, alternating between modelling a worked example with the class and setting a minimally different problem for the students to solve (see Figure 2.1). A minimally different problem is one that is similar in terms of cognitive load (no easier or harder).

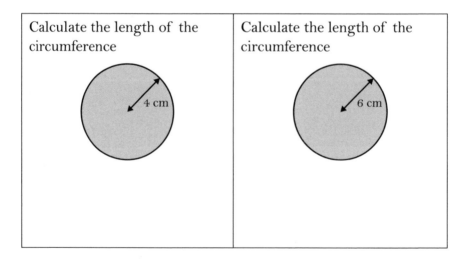

Figure 2.1. An example of minimally different problems

During explanation, this is best done by splitting the board in half. The worked example is live modelled (write each step as you go rather than having each step prepared) on one side and the problem for the students to solve is on the other (as in Figure 2.2).

An important point to note here is not to reveal the problem for the students to solve until after you have live modelled the worked example. This will ensure that the students fully attend to the worked example, rather than rushing ahead to solve their own problem. Asking students to complete the minimally different problem on mini whiteboards is the best way to gain whole-class feedback to determine whether we need another worked example pair or whether they are ready to practise independently.

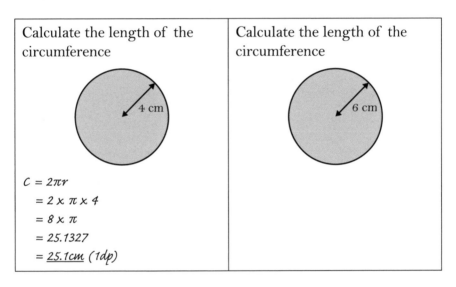

Figure 2.2. Using worked example pairs

This strategy has lots of moving parts. Here's a summary of how to use worked example pairs to reduce the cognitive load placed on your students:

♦ For each example you wish to model, pair it with a minimally different problem for students to solve.

♦ Reveal the paired problem to students only *after* the worked example has been live modelled.

♦ Check all students' understanding by asking them to solve their problem using mini whiteboards.

You can supercharge the impact of your worked example pairs by adding silent modelling (see strategy 5 in this chapter).

Incomplete Worked Examples

Another way to use worked examples is to give students an incomplete worked example (alternatively referred to as a completion task) in which one or more step is missing. This strategy utilises the idea that the gradual reduction or fading of instructional guidance as levels of learner expertise increase is more effective than abruptly switching from worked examples to un-scaffolded problems.[14]

Calculate $171 \div 3$ $$0\,5\,\boxed{}$$ $$3\,\overline{\left|17\,{}^{2}1\right.}$$	**Solve $2x + 1 > 7$** $$2x + 1 > 7$$ $$2x > 6$$ $$\boxed{}$$
Solve $x^2 + 3 = -4x$ $$x^2 + 3 = -4x$$ $$x^2 + 4x + 3 = 0$$ $$(x + 1)(x + 3) = 0$$ $$\boxed{}$$ $\underline{x = -1 \text{ and } x = -3}$	**Find the mean of 3, 5, 6, 6, 7, 8 and 8** $$\boxed{}$$ $43 \div 7 = 6.1$ (to 1 decimal place)

Figure 2.3. Examples of incomplete worked examples

The missing step(s) can be at the beginning, middle or end of the worked example, although there is some evidence to suggest that *backward* fading – whereby the last step or steps are omitted (as in the first two examples in Figure 2.3) are more effective, especially when paired with student self-explanation (see strategy 12 in this chapter).[15]

Incorrect Worked Examples

Incorrect worked examples are literally just that: a worked example that is incorrect (see Figure 2.4). They are an immensely powerful way to identify and address any misconceptions that may be lurking.

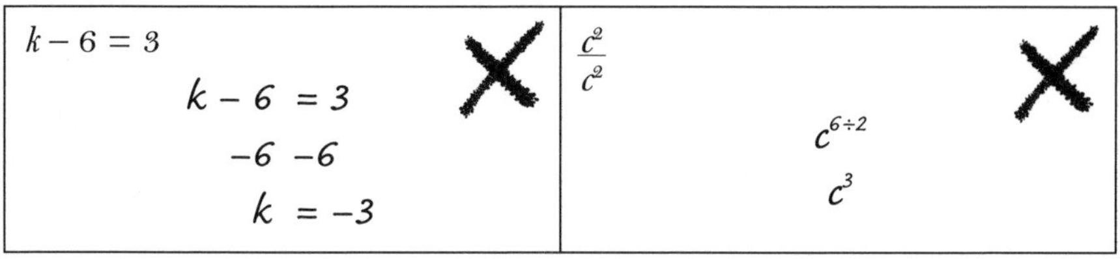

$k - 6 = 3$

$$k - 6 = 3$$
$$-6 \ -6$$
$$k = -3$$

$\dfrac{c^2}{c^2}$

$$c^{6 \div 2}$$
$$c^3$$

Figure 2.4. Incorrect worked examples © SERP Institute[16]

There is an understandable concern that using incorrect worked examples may cause confusion and introduce misconceptions that students did not previously have. However, it has been shown that incorrect worked examples help students to recognise incorrect procedures and think about the differences between them and the correct procedures, which can increase their conceptual and procedural knowledge.[17]

One crucial element in avoiding potential confusion is to ensure the students know that an incorrect example is incorrect. Highlight them by using a large red cross and a red border to indicate when an example is incorrect and, conversely, use a large green tick and green border for correct examples (when using worked example pairs, for example). Explicitly verbalising that an example is incorrect (or correct) before discussing the example is also important: "This example is incorrect."

Incorrect worked examples are fairly easy to create (assuming you know what misconceptions your students are likely to have[18]):

1 Identify *one* misconception you wish to address (do not be tempted to address more than one in an example as this greatly reduces the effectiveness).

2 Create an incorrect worked example that exemplifies this misconception.

3 Add a red cross and red border so the students know it is incorrect.

4 Use a student's name and state that they are incorrect: "Peps solved this problem *incorrectly* ..."

Luckily, there is a pool of readymade incorrect worked examples to draw on (for algebra), courtesy of AlgebraByExample.[19] Their materials make use of the worked example pair strategy by teaming an incorrect worked example with a problem for the students to complete. They also harness the power of student self-explanation, so that students are prompted to make sense of what they are learning (there is more on this at the end of the chapter).

Helaina tried to simplify this expression, but she *didn't* do it correctly. Here is her first step:

$$5 - 4x + 2$$

$$5 - 4x + 2$$

$$4x - 5 + 2$$

What did Helaina do wrong in her first step?

Would it have been okay to write $5 + 2 - 4x$? Explain why or why not.

Your turn:

$$12x + 4 - 5x$$

Figure 2.5. Incorrect worked example pair with student self-explanation © SERP Institute[20]

Incorrect worked examples can place a strain on working memory because there are so many features to attend to: students need to locate the error, create a correct model and identify why the incorrect worked example was wrong. This load can be reduced by scaffolding the task – for example, by pointing out which is the incorrect step (as in Figure 2.5).

Crucial to students' success is good prior knowledge and exposure to correct worked examples.

Correct and Incorrect Worked Examples

Another way to employ incorrect worked examples is to use them in conjunction with correct worked examples so the students are able to compare them directly (as in Figure 2.6). This can reduce the cognitive load created by sharing incorrect worked examples on their own.

Factorise $x^2 - 4$		
Chen factorised the expression **correctly** ✓	Lucy factorised the expression **incorrectly** ✗	Vicky factorised the expression **incorrectly** ✗
$x^2 - 4$ $= (x - 2)(x + 2)$	$x^2 - 4$ $= (x - 2)(x - 2)$	$x^2 - 4$ $= x(x - 4)$

Figure 2.6. Correct and incorrect worked examples

To encourage student self-explanation (see strategy 12), some example questions to ask are:

◆ How can you show that the solutions from Lucy and Vicky are incorrect?

◆ What advice would you give to Lucy and Vicky to help them avoid factorising this type of problem incorrectly in the future?

◆ How can you check that Chen factorised this expression correctly?

◆ What strategy would you use to factorise this expression, and why did you choose that strategy?

Strategy Comparison Worked Examples

This strategy uses worked examples of the same problem solved in different ways, so that a comparison of different approaches can be made (see Figure 2.7). Comparing different strategies that yield the correct solution can help to deepen students' conceptual understanding and enable them to notice similarities and differences between problem structures and solution strategies. Asking students to compare strategies may be more conducive to learning than asking them to study individual strategies because comparison activities enable students to reference their prior knowledge of one strategy to learn new strategies.[21]

Find 35% of 120	
Katie's solution	*Louise's solution*
$0.35 \times 120 = \underline{42}$	50% of 120 is 60 so 25% of 120 is 30 10% of 120 is 12 35% is 25% + 10% 30 + 12 = $\underline{42}$

Calculate $2\frac{2}{3} + 3\frac{1}{4}$	
Cath's solution	*Bernard's solution*
$\frac{8}{3} + \frac{13}{4}$ $= \frac{32}{12} + \frac{39}{12}$ $= \frac{71}{12}$ $= 5\frac{11}{12}$	$(2 + 3) + \left(\frac{2}{3} + \frac{1}{4}\right)$ $= 5 + \left(\frac{8}{12} + \frac{3}{12}\right)$ $= 5 + \frac{11}{12}$ $= 5\frac{11}{12}$

Solve $5(x + 3) = 45$	
Mullen's solution	*Maimie's solution*
$5x + 15 = 45$ $5x = 30$ $x = \underline{6}$	$x + 3 = 9$ $x = \underline{6}$

Solve these simultaneous equations $3x + 4y = 25$ and $x + 2y = 11$

Shaun's solution	*Andy's solution*
$3x + 4y = 25$ ... A $x + 2y = 11$ ... B $3x + 4y = 25$ ... A $\underline{3x + 6y = 33}$ ... 3B $2y = 8$ ... 3B − A $y = 4$ $x + 2(4) = 11$ ... In B $x + 8 = 11$ $x = 3$ $3(3) + 4(4) = 9 + 16 = 25$ ... In A $\underline{x = 3 \text{ and } y = 4}$	$3x + 4y = 25$ ... A $x + 2y = 11$ ... B $x = 11 - 2y$ ... B $3(11 - 2y) + 4y = 25$ ... B in A $33 - 6y + 4y = 25$ $6y - 4y = 33 - 25$ $2y = 8$ $y = 4$ $x + 2(4) = 11$ ... In B $x + 8 = 11$ $x = 3$ $3(3) + 4(4) = 9 + 16 = 25$ ... In A $\underline{x = 3 \text{ and } y = 4}$

Find the area of this compound shape

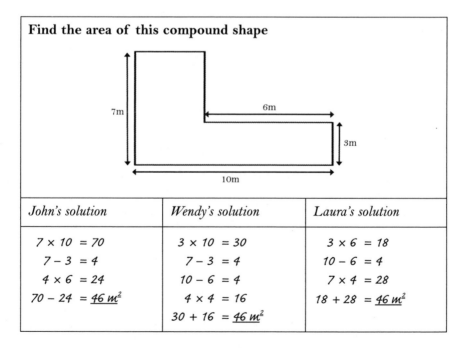

John's solution	*Wendy's solution*	*Laura's solution*
$7 \times 10 = 70$ $7 - 3 = 4$ $4 \times 6 = 24$ $70 - 24 = \underline{46 \, m^2}$	$3 \times 10 = 30$ $7 - 3 = 4$ $10 - 6 = 4$ $4 \times 4 = 16$ $30 + 16 = \underline{46 \, m^2}$	$3 \times 6 = 18$ $10 - 6 = 4$ $7 \times 4 = 28$ $18 + 28 = \underline{46 \, m^2}$

Figure 2.7. Examples of using worked examples to compare different solution strategies

When presenting students with worked examples in this way, prompt them to compare the different solutions by asking, "How do these strategies all give the same solution?"

This strategy offers five different ways to harness the power of worked examples. In terms of which one to use when, worked example pairs should be deployed initially to help explain a concept. The effectiveness of the remaining types of worked examples tend to rely on the students having been exposed to correct worked examples and so are more flexible in their use. They can be used in any order and in a multitude of ways – for example, to check prior knowledge, during practice, as homework or as exit tickets to inform next steps.

Note that while this strategy promotes the understanding and use of multiple solutions, it is not necessary that students are fluent in all of the different methods for solving a given problem.

3. Concept/Non-concept

The *variation theory* of learning points to variation as being a necessary component in teaching in order for students to notice what is to be learned.[22] One of the principles of variation theory is that seeing differences precedes seeing sameness: if you have never heard another language, you cannot possibly understand what Chinese is simply by listening to different people speaking Chinese. Nor can you understand what a linear equation is by looking only at linear equations.[23]

Imagine a teacher trying to convey the meaning of a concept to her students. It is highly likely that she would use examples to exemplify what the concept is. For instance, if she was trying to help her students to understand what a radius is, she would probably show them a circle with a radius. What she might *not* do is show them what a radius isn't. But it turns out that showing students what something isn't is an incredibly effective way of helping them to understand what it is.

The concept/non-concept strategy has been a revelation to me. It is beautifully simple yet incredibly powerful. It helps the students to gain a deeper understanding of a concept through being shown examples of what the concept is (concept) and what the concept is not (non-concept). It works because it encourages students to attend to the details that define a concept. This means that they have a better mental model of what it is.

It can even help the students to create their own mathematical definitions. It's a great strategy – even Ofsted thinks so![24]

Unsurprisingly, it is best explained through examples. Consider this scenario with a young student. They are shown the shape on the left in Figure 2.8 and are asked what it is. They don't know. Further exploration reveals that they don't know because their mental model of a triangle is the one on the right. They recognise triangles that are like the one on the right but struggle to identify those that we would call 'boundary cases'. By boundary cases, I mean examples that are close to the limit of a definition but furthest from the standard case (another example would be a hexagon in the shape of an 'L').

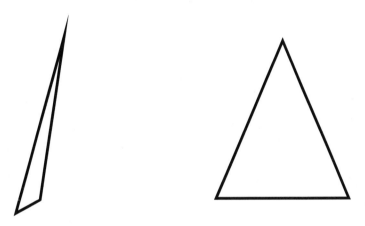

Figure 2.8. Examples of a boundary case and a standard case representation of a triangle

A lack of familiarity with boundary cases is replicated across the curriculum. Students struggle to identify an irregular hexagon as a hexagon because too often they only meet a regular hexagon. They struggle to understand an equation as being two things that are equal, such as $10 + 1 = 2 + 3 + 6$, and instead recognise only the standard cases – for example, $2x + 1 = 6$. It is unlikely that students would correctly identify a diameter as also being a chord.

Concept/non-concept helps us to address this problem by providing a structure to better define concepts from the outset. Let's return to the triangle scenario. If we asked the student to define a triangle, what might they have said? I suspect it would have been something along the lines of, "A triangle is a shape with three sides."

Now, imagine our student is shown each of the images in Figure 2.9 in turn and is told whether or not it is a triangle. If we then ask them to define a triangle, they would probably talk about it having *three sides* that are *straight* and the shape needing to be *closed* (although they might not use the word 'closed' they are likely to convey some sense of the term). Their definition would certainly be more sophisticated than their first attempt. Now, if presented with a boundary case triangle they would be much more likely to identify it correctly.

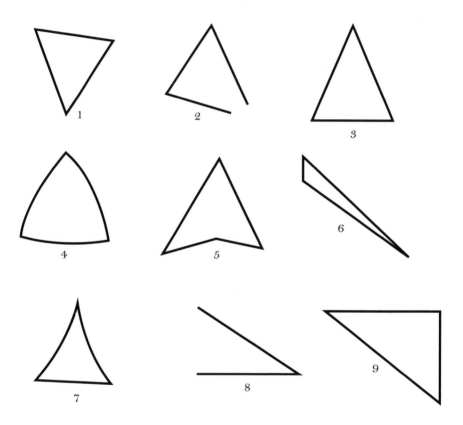

Figure 2.9. A sequence of concept/non-concept examples for a triangle

Figure 2.10 applies concept/non-concept to prime numbers – the defini-tion of which my students often struggled to understand and remember. The figure illustrates a suitably broad set of examples that make the link to the number of factors.

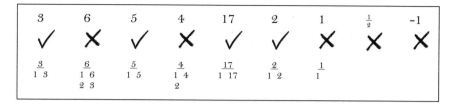

Figure 2.10. A sequence of concept/non-concept examples for prime numbers

To avoid overload, share one example at a time, narrating as follows:

---

3 has factors 1 and 3. 3 is a prime number.

6 has factors 1, 6, 2 and 3. 6 is not a prime number.

5 has factors 1 and 5. 5 is a prime number.

4 has factors 1, 4 and 2. 4 is not a prime number.

etc.

To further help our students to think about the differences between the examples we can:

1   Pause at any point during the sequence of examples and ask the students to decide what they think a prime number is. For each remaining example, ask them to predict using mini whiteboards whether they think the numbers are prime or not.

2   Pause at any point during the sequence of examples and ask the students to write down a description of what they think a prime number is. Continue to work through the remaining examples, asking them to check if their description still stands, adjusting or adding to it if necessary.

3   Share all of the examples and then ask the students to list and share the characteristics of a prime number (the Frayer model in Figure 2.12 is an effective tool to record this).

Note that at no point in this process has the teacher explicitly defined a prime number.

Each of the examples in Figure 2.10 has been chosen carefully (unlike those in our 'glerm' example at the start of the chapter). 4 has been selected because it has an odd number of factors, thus avoiding students creating a mis-rule that prime numbers are numbers with an even number of factors. 17 is chosen because it has two digits – to prevent the students from creating a mis-rule that prime numbers are single digit numbers. Notice that boundary cases are explored towards the end of the set of examples, which will lead to rich discussion about the factor(s) of 1 and fractional and negative 'factors'. This process should lead the students to a deeper understanding of what defines a prime number. Use green ticks and red crosses to ensure clarity around which examples represent the concept and which do not.

Finally, in Figure 2.11, we use concept/non-concept examples to define a radius. The last example is a boundary case: not one radius but two, with a special name – a diameter.

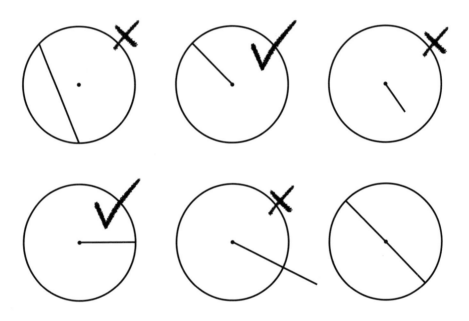

Figure 2.11. A sequence of concept/non-concept examples for a radius

The Frayer model is an effective tool to help the students order their thoughts (see Figure 2.12). It provides a structure for them to record their thinking either during or after the concept/non-concept sequence.

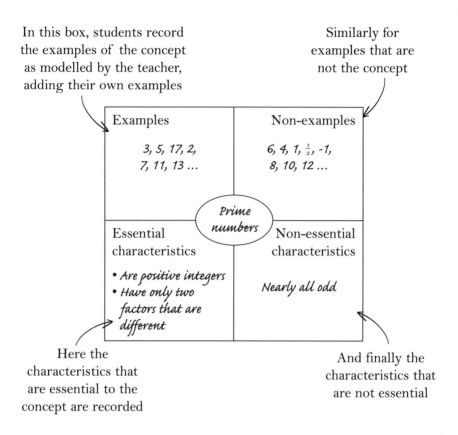

In this box, students record the examples of the concept as modelled by the teacher, adding their own examples

Similarly for examples that are not the concept

Examples

3, 5, 17, 2,
7, 11, 13 ...

Non-examples

6, 4, 1, $\frac{1}{2}$, -1,
8, 10, 12 ...

Prime numbers

Essential characteristics

• Are positive integers
• Have only two factors that are different

Non-essential characteristics

Nearly all odd

Here the characteristics that are essential to the concept are recorded

And finally the characteristics that are not essential

Figure 2.12. Using the Frayer model with prime numbers during or after use of concept/non-concept

The scope of topics for which concept/non-concept can be used is plentiful; in a nutshell, it can be used for any mathematical concept. However, it doesn't work beyond concepts – for example, finding a non-concept example for adding fractions is nonsensical because adding fractions is not a concept.[25]

Strategies for Tell

Language in maths is more important than I ever imagined. As the National Centre for Excellence in the Teaching of Mathematics observes, "Learners do not know mathematics until they can 'speak' it. Effective teaching therefore focuses on the communicative aspects of mathematics by developing oral and written mathematical language."[26] The 'strategies for tell' remind us that the language we use with our students – and that they use in response – is important.

4. Less is More

My Achilles heel is that I talk too much. This leads to me over-narrating worked examples and asking too many questions. I used to think that this helped my students gain a deeper understanding, but in hindsight it is clear that it was overwhelming them and causing cognitive overload. In addition, my explanations tended to overrun, impacting on the other phases of the lesson.

We need to be economical with our language for four main reasons: so that students attend to the most important parts, to reduce cognitive load, to make efficient use of learning time and to give students a better under-standing of how long it really takes to solve a problem. Dani Quinn, the head of maths at Michaela Community School, points out that we often do so much talking when modelling an example that the students, under-standably, think procedures take much longer and are more complex than they actually are.[27] Taking several minutes to model solving one area problem sets them up with the belief that it will take them equally as long.

This strategy is simply about being more aware of the length of our narrations and asking ourselves whether we are being concise with our language. As the saying goes, less is more. Rehearsal is an important part of this process. Actors rehearse to ensure they are able to deliver their best performance; reviewing our explanations will allow us to do the same. Alternatively, we can analyse the brevity of our explanations by videoing this part of our lesson or by asking a colleague to observe and feed back. This allows us to unpick which parts of our narration, and which of the questions we ask the students, are necessary and pertinent. Repeating this process will make our explanations more succinct and effective.

5. Silence is Golden

This strategy is about silent modelling, meaning that when you model a worked example, you literally do so in silence. There are several compel-ling reasons to use silent modelling – the most compelling being that it helps us to manage cognitive load by focusing student attention solely on each step of the worked example without the distraction of a narrative. It also sets a more realistic expectation of how long it takes to solve a problem.

Silent modelling is most effective when paired with worked example pairs (see strategy 2). First, model an example silently, as if you were solving the problem yourself, pausing briefly after each line of working. Then ask the students to complete a minimally different problem using mini white-boards. For more complex worked examples, it may be helpful to invite the students to ask for clarifications or to repeat the model with narration before they complete their minimally different problem.

What is most revealing about this strategy is how little we need to say.

6. Speak Proper

Rachel's Year 3 class were working on a data-handling project for which they were counting sweets. One student, for whom English was a second language, had grouped his sweets by colour. Rachel asked him to draw a table. When she returned he had drawn a piece of furniture.[28]

Maths has a wonderful technical lexicon which provides us with a way of describing and defining concepts and processes so that we can reach a common understanding. Yet it contains two distinct groups of words, each of which are problematic for different reasons. First is the group of words that exist only in our subject (e.g. integer, hypotenuse) and, as such, have a single definition. While having a single meaning is helpful in terms of clarity, it can be difficult for students to fully master their understanding because the likelihood of encountering these words in everyday conversation or in the media is low.

More problematic are the second group – those terms that share the same spelling and pronunciation as other words but have different meanings (polysemous words). Take the word 'similar', for example. Generally, if we say something is similar we mean that it is nearly the same but not quite. Saying 'I have a similar coat' to someone could mean that it is the same colour but a different style, or that they are both long in length but different in all other aspects. In maths, however, the word similar has a very specific meaning. Likewise, if you asked students to 'construct an expression with a product' in their English lesson, the outcome would be very different to what they might create in maths.

The problem with polysemous words is that on hearing them, students will recall their default definition – and in most cases, it will not be the mathematical definition. So, when we ask students to visualise a table they may well think of a piece of furniture, or when we ask them to add a key to a statistical diagram, a house key may be their first thought. Consequently, when students meet terms in maths that have more than one meaning, especially for the first time, we need to acknowledge these multiple meanings, be explicit about their meaning in maths and clarify how these definitions differ.

Chord, Complex, Constant, Digit, Even, Expand, Expression, Factor, Function, Imaginary, Inequality, Key, Mean, Model, Natural, Negative, Odd, Order, Point, Power, Prime, Product, Radius, Range, Rational, Real, Root, Scale, Sector, Series, Table, Term, Translate, Volume

---

Figure 2.13. Examples of polysemous words in the maths lexicon – there are many more

When I first starting teaching, I thought that I could make maths more accessible and understandable to my students by allowing them (and occasionally me) to use informal language. 'Top number' was acceptable for numerator and 'plug in' for substitute. Alongside this, I repeated phrases that I had been taught without considering the implications – for example, when rounding I would say, "round to the nearest hundred", instead of "round to the nearest multiple of one hundred", which is far easier to understand.

The problem with informal language is that students gain less exposure to the correct mathematical language. This can restrict their understanding when these ideas are built upon later and may lead to confusion in formal assessments when precise language is used. Equally, informal language often relies on superficial features such as the position of symbols on the page rather than the underlying mathematical operations.

Despite this, informal language does have a role to play as a bridge from the concrete (i.e. familiar words) to the abstract, technical language. While it is fine to use informal language in the classroom to help define a concept, it is necessary for the students to know and use precise mathematical terms.[29] With regular use, both by teacher and student, it is more likely that students will add the word to their vocabulary.

Finally, here are some examples of how default language, which lacks precision, can cause confusion and increase the risk of misconceptions (Table 2.1). It is far from an exhaustive list.

Table 2.1. Examples of imprecise and precise mathematical language[30]

The problematic saying ...	The problem it creates	Instead, say ...
Carrying or *borrowing* when adding or subtracting, respectively	This language refers to procedures.	Exchanging – e.g. *exchange 10 ones for 1 ten, 1 ten for 10 ones, 10 tens for 1 hundred,* etc.
Plug in the 2 or *Put 2 in* when substituting numbers in algebra	There is a risk that students will be unfamiliar with the formal language of maths.	*Substitute 2 for x*
Top number and *bottom number* to describe parts of a fraction	Suggests that the numerator and denominator are separate numbers when, in fact, the fraction is itself one number.	Use *numerator* and *denominator*

The problematic saying ...	The problem it creates	Instead, say ...
a is for apples	This embeds the misconception that a letter represents an object (rather than a variable). It may appear to help when collecting like terms, but it can lead to misconceptions in cases such as $3a + 4a + 2$. Students are likely to ask themselves 'Plus 2 what?' and most probably infer they must be apples too.	*Let a be the number of apples in a bag* ($3a$ is then 3 bags of apples). Or *a is the weight of an apple in grammes.* Or, staying clear of apples, *a is the unknown length of this line* ⟵――――――――⟶ a
Do the opposite to each side when solving equations	This is informal language.	*Use the inverse operation*
KFC (keep, flip, change) when dividing by a fraction	This language is informal and refers to procedures.	*Multiply by the reciprocal* so that students gain a deeper understanding of what is happening mathematically e.g. $\frac{1}{2} \div \frac{3}{5} = \left(\frac{1}{2} \times \frac{5}{3}\right) \div \left(\frac{3}{5} \times \frac{5}{3}\right) = \frac{5}{6} \div 1 = \frac{5}{6}$
The numbers cancel out	This language refers to procedures.	*The numbers add to give zero* (or form a zero pair). Or *The numbers divide to give one*

The problematic saying ...	The problem it creates	Instead, say ...
Which is bigger? when referring to numbers	Numbers should not be described as being bigger because bigger is associated with size and shape.	*Greater* (because it is associated with quantity)
Stating that a number divides *evenly* into another number e.g. *5 divides evenly into 45*	The word *even* has a different meaning and is therefore being misused.	*45 can be divided by 5 without remainder* Or *5 is a factor of 45*

In summary, to ensure that we develop our students' mathematical vocabulary and understanding of such, we need to:

♦ Define maths vocabulary clearly (e.g. using concept/non-concept).

♦ Explicitly acknowledge and address the conflict caused when words are polysemous.

♦ Model the meticulous and consistent use of maths vocabulary, repeating important terms at least three times.

♦ Expect students to use mathematical language.

♦ Build in regular opportunities for the students to practise the retrieval of vocabulary, definitions and representations (e.g. through use of flashcards or by using strategy 8 in Chapter 4).

Strategies for Bridging Concrete to Abstract

We cannot avoid the fact that maths is a difficult subject to learn due, in part, to its abstract nature. In order for the students to be able to access abstract concepts, such as algebra, we need to provide a bridge that helps them to understand. Each of the strategies below help students to make connections between the concrete and the abstract.

7. Concrete, Pictorial, Abstract

My most memorable light-bulb moment in maths occurred when I was already a teacher.[31] I was shown the pictorial form of completing the square (Figure 2.14) and it blew my mind! Prior to that, throughout my 17 years of maths education, I had only met the abstract form $(x + \frac{b}{2})^2 - (\frac{b}{2})^2$ which, quite frankly, I didn't understand and was reluctant to use. This revelation not only changed my understanding, but it changed the way I taught solving quadratic equations and, for me, hints at the power of using concrete and pictorial representations to bridge the abstract.

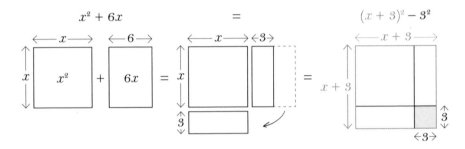

Figure 2.14. Visual representation of completing the square

The most common approach to building this bridge is to move between concrete, pictorial and abstract forms (commonly known as CPA). *Concrete* means grounding the concept in a familiar and accessible form, often by using manipulatives (i.e. "physical objects that pupils or teachers can touch and move, used to support the teaching and learning of mathematics"[32]), *pictorial* is the concept represented in a diagram and *abstract* refers to the formal use of mathematical symbols and notation. For example, when young children first learn about multiplication, they often create groups or arrays using counters (concrete). If we represented this array as a series of dots, this would provide a pictorial representation. Abstraction is the problem written using numbers and operations.

CPA provides a scaffold which can be removed over time. Initially, it is likely that all three forms will be used. Gradually, the concrete/manipulative form can be removed and then the pictorial. In our example, once the students' understanding of multiplication is secure, they will no longer need to rely on the concrete form. That said, it might be useful to return to it occasionally.

Note that while there is evidence that manipulatives can help students to understand complex ideas, caution is urged with their use. When they are not used well, manipulatives can actually make it harder for students to learn. The Education Endowment Foundation advises: "ensure that there is a clear rationale for using a particular manipulative or representation to teach a specific mathematical concept".[33] One of the barriers faced in secondary schools is our lack of familiarity with manipulatives – we must access training and take time to practise before presenting them to students.

There are many different types of manipulatives available, including online versions to model with the whole class (of which Jonathan Hall's MathsBot website has a multitude[34]); multipurpose ones, such as Cuisenaire rods and multilink cubes, which serve lots of different topics; and specific ones such as hula models for circle theorems[35] or shoe boxes for Pythagoras' theorem and trigonometry in three dimensions.

Let's consider what the CPA approach might look like in algebra – the most abstract concept of all. When we begin to build new ideas in algebra we can tether to the concrete by using algebra tiles. These can be bought as a set or made from card. They are comprised of three distinct sized and coloured tiles with the areas used to represent algebraic terms and numbers:

1   A yellow unit square with side length 1 representing 1.

2   A green rectangle with an unknown side length x and known side length 1 with area x.[36]

3   A blue square with unknown side length x with area x^2.

The underside of each of the tiles is red to represent negative terms: -1, -x and -x^2 respectively.

With these three tiles it is possible to create and manipulate expressions, including expanding and factorising, and solve linear and quadratic equations.[37] Initially we can use the tiles as the concrete form alongside the abstract – when we use the tiles to create algebraic models we also represent this using algebraic notation. Over time, we can move to pictorial representations of the tiles, and eventually we can remove the scaffold completely and work only in the abstract. This process is summarised in Figure 2.15. Note that it may be necessary to return to the concrete or pictorial at times.

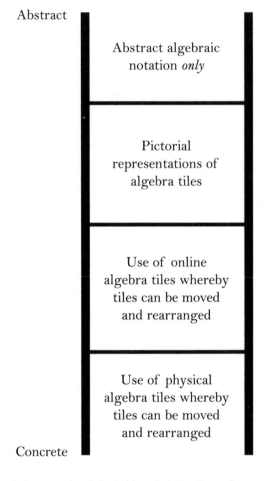

Figure 2.15. An example of the ladder of abstraction – from concrete to abstract

Remarkably, algebra tiles can also be used when working with directed numbers. Examples of this can be seen in Figure 2.16: the lighter tiles represent the yellow unit square with value +1 and the darker tiles the red unit square with value -1.

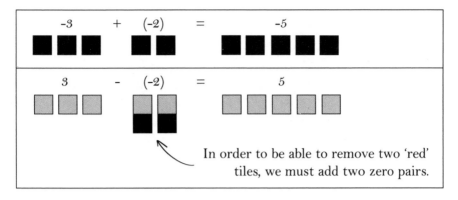

Figure 2.16. Using algebra tiles when adding and subtracting directed numbers

8. Representations

Given that the Education Endowment Foundation has recommended the use of manipulatives and representations, we now turn our focus to representations.[38] When we use the term 'representation' in maths we mean "a particular form in which mathematics is presented".[39] For example, an expression can be represented in its algebraic form as a diagram using areas, in a table of values or in words (see Figure 2.17). Other representations include, but are not limited to, graphs, number lines, double number lines and bar models. Representations are recommended as a powerful tool for problem solving.[40]

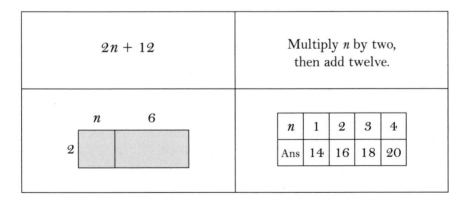

Figure 2.17. Example representations of an algebraic expression[41]

Bar modelling

Bar modelling is increasing in popularity due to its versatility and its effective use in Singapore classrooms. Bars are used to represent known and unknown values which can be compared and manipulated to find a solution to a given problem. Bar modelling can be applied to many topics (algebra tiles are generalisations of the bar model to support algebraic thinking) and is a powerful tool for problem solving.[42] The Education Endowment Foundation and National Centre for Excellence in the Teaching of Mathematics both promote the use of bar modelling; however, as with manipulatives, we need to ensure that we access training and take time to practise before presenting them to students.

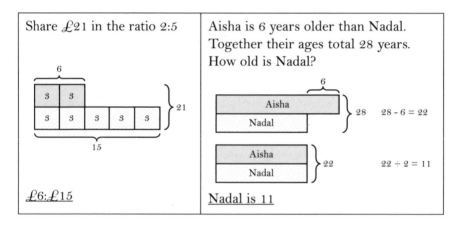

Figure 2.18. Examples of using bar models to solve problems

Should you wish to use bar models, aim to consider the following points:

♦ Use an online bar modelling tool to live model with the students. This can also be used to produce images for slides and problems.[43]

♦ If the students are not familiar with bar modelling, you may wish to start by introducing a concrete form (e.g. manipulating strips of paper by cutting).

♦ There is no universal agreement on how to label or format bar models so it is vital that a decision is made within the department to ensure consistency. Talk to feeder schools about their use of bar modelling.

Number lines

Number lines can sometimes get forgotten in secondary schools, despite their power. Using number lines means that students do not need to hold as much information in their working memory, allowing us to better manage their cognitive load. Figure 2.19 demonstrates how we might use a number line to expose the common misconception that when adding fractions, we add the numerators and then add the denominators. By representing $\frac{1}{2}$, $\frac{1}{6}$ and $\frac{2}{8}$ on a number line it becomes clear that $\frac{1}{2} + \frac{1}{6} \neq \frac{2}{8}$.

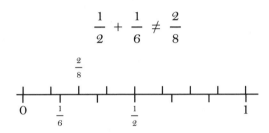

Figure 2.19. Using a number line to expose misconceptions

What is particularly interesting about this example is that when working with fractions, we often tend to default to using shapes – generally circles or rectangles, depending on the denominator. Positioning them on a number line can be a much easier way for students to directly compare different fractions.

Number lines can also be used to develop students' understanding of the nature of decimal numbers and rounding.[44]

Finally, there is promising evidence that *comparing* and discussing different representations (see Figure 2.17 for an example) can help pupils to develop conceptual understanding. That said, a word of caution is required: using too many representations at once may cause confusion and hinder learning.[45] A useful rule of thumb is to start with two representations and only build on this if there is a compelling reason to use more.

9. Dynamic Representations

Dynamic representations – representations that we can move or manipulate – are one of the ways in which technology can really enhance the learning of maths. We can use them in two ways:

1 To convey movement (e.g. when studying transformations).

2 To demonstrate visual exemplification (i.e. informal proof) by manipulating and comparing different representations (see Figures 2.20 and 2.21).

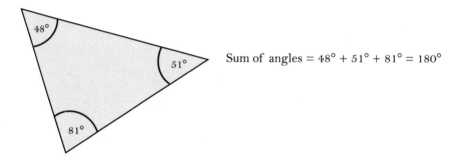

Sum of angles $= 48° + 51° + 81° = 180°$

Figure 2.20. Exemplifying that the angles in a triangle sum to 180°. The size of the angles can be changed by dragging the vertices while the total remains at 180°

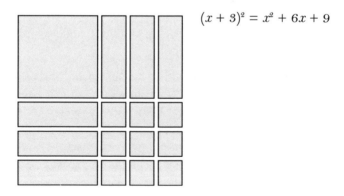

$(x + 3)^2 = x^2 + 6x + 9$

Figure 2.21. Comparing the pictorial and algebraic forms of perfect squares. A slider tool can be used to change both forms simultaneously[46]

There are some excellent platforms that allow us to create these representations ourselves, such as www.geogebra.org and www.desmos.

com. Thankfully, there is no need for us to do the legwork because www.
mathimation.co.uk has built and shared many useful dynamic representations, while a search on GeoGebra yields many results created by
wonderful maths teachers from all over the world.

10. Gesture

Gestures are a non-verbal form of communication that we use every day.
We do this by moving parts of the body, usually the head or hands, to
express an idea or meaning. Many gestures are in common usage because
they are universally understood, such as thumbs-up, okay and those used
by one driver when another driver demonstrates poor driving skills! As
babies, we understand gestures before words, so our ability to interpret
them is hardwired from a very young age.

Gesture is used in the classroom in the sense that we all use movement to
some extent when speaking. However, if used purposefully, gesture has
the potential to improve outcomes for our students. One observable way
in which it does this is by focusing their visual attention on important
features. However, recent research suggests that the beneficial effects of
gesture come not merely from its ability to guide visual attention, but also
from the ability to synchronise with speech and affect what learners glean
from that speech.[47] There is evidence to suggest that gesture enhances the
learning of abstract concepts and affects how learning is consolidated
over time.[48]

Table 2.2. A summary of some ideas for using gesture in the classroom to aid
understanding

Context	Gesture
Substitution	Pointing at the variable and number to be substituted
Solving equations	Use both hands open and move them up and down to convey balance. Use the thumb and forefinger held apart to convey each weighing scale and hold them below each side of the equation.

Context	Gesture
Graphs	Use straight arms to show straight lines. Use bent arms for quadratics and cubics.
Increase or decrease	Pointing up or down.
Growth or decay	Use an inclined/declined forearm.
Listing steps	Hold up the number of fingers as you describe each step.
Size	Use the thumb and forefinger close together to indicate tiny and hands wide apart to indicate large.
Comparing representations	Point to the parts of each representation that are the same. For example, if comparing a straight line graph and its equation, point to the y intercept of each.

11. Analogy

Analogy enables us to explain unfamiliar concepts by comparing them to familiar concepts that share common characteristics. An example in maths is the comparison of the concept of perimeter with the length of a fence that encloses a field. Here the unfamiliar concept is perimeter. We tether this to the prior knowledge that students have of what a fence is, what it means for a fence to fully enclose a field and what the length of the fence represents. In doing so, we are helping the students to understand that the perimeter of a shape shares a useful characteristic with the length of a fence around a field. Given that we know new knowledge needs to be tethered to existing knowledge, this makes analogy an immensely powerful tool for explanation and provides a bridge from concrete to abstract.

However, analogy can be tricky to use well. Consider our perimeter example. If we said "perimeter is like a fence" we would be drawing the students' attention to a fence. The students may think about the fence colour or materials. Perhaps their imagined fence continues into the distance and does not border a closed area. Either way, the students are not thinking about the analogy in the way we want them to. We need to draw their attention to the two key features: the total length of the fence and the fact that the fence is closed. Perimeter is not like a fence; it is like the total length of a fence that completely encloses a field. Using the term 'perimeter fence' can help, although in my experience students are not familiar with this phrase. If students are unfamiliar with the familiar part of an analogy, it will fail.

Assuming the students are familiar with a fence enclosing a field, the perimeter analogy works because it draws on existing knowledge to ensure they have a greater understanding of the new concept. However, some analogies are used to *replace* understanding – these are best avoided. An example from my past teaching is the 'adding or taking hot/cold from a room' analogy for adding and subtracting directed numbers. It is a poor analogy because it is a shortcut. It does not lead to greater understanding and can lead to confusion and misapplication when we are faced with, for example, -2 + -5. In this scenario, it would be better to avoid analogy and instead use a CPA approach with algebra tiles.

When considering using analogies, there are several principles that can help us to make them especially effective: familiarity, vividness, making the connection clear and continuing to reinforce the analogy.[49] In Table 2.3 we see these principles in action for our perimeter example and for an analogy which likens linear equations to balancing scales.

Table 2.3. Applying the principles of analogy to perimeter and linear equations

Principle	**Perimeter analogy**	**Linear equations analogy**
Familiarity	Students know what a fence enclosing a field is.	Students know what a set of balancing scales are.
Vividness	Tell a story about taking a walk along the length of the fence.	Have a set of scales for the students to see.
Making connection clear (similar features)	Display a shape and trace the perimeter as if walking the length of the shape.	Write the two sides of the equation over the two sides of a drawing of a set of scales.

Principle	Perimeter analogy	Linear equations analogy
Reinforce	Regularly refer to perimeter as the length of a fence enclosing a field.	Refer to the scales at appropriate times when an equation is solved.

One of the confusing things about analogies in maths is that they can take many forms. Our perimeter example is an *informal* verbal analogy. Willingham suggests that manipulatives also serve as analogies, whereby the things manipulated are symbols of the new, to-be-understood idea.[50] There also exists *formal* analogy in the form 'x is to y as a is to b'. A simple example of this, which can be a good place to start in the classroom, is 'puppy is to dog as kitten is to cat'. This type of analogy is rarely used in maths but can provide an interesting way to explore relationships. Below are some examples in which knowledge of a familiar concept is used to aid understanding of a less familiar concept which students often have difficulty understanding:

♦ Perimeter is to rectangle as circumference is to circle.

♦ Ruler is to line as protractor is to angle.

♦ Centimetres are to metres as inches are to feet.

♦ Rectangle is to cuboid as circle is to cylinder.

♦ Unicycle is to bicycle is to tricycle as monomial is to binomial is to trinomial.

♦ 0.5 is to $\frac{1}{2}$ as 0.1 is to $\frac{1}{10}$.

The remaining two strategies look at how we can encourage our students to better explain ideas to themselves and the importance of being consistent in the methods we choose to teach.

12. Student Self-Explanation

Imagine you are on a professional development course. The trainer is talking and you are taking notes which list the main ideas in a way that helps you to understand (rather than writing word for word what the trainer is saying). You are listening to the trainer, analysing the content and summarising the ideas. Notice that you are not explaining to a colleague sitting next to you or answering a question the trainer has asked. You are self-explaining, the goal of which is to make sense of what you are reading or hearing, which is an important part of the learning process.

Unfortunately, students do not tend to self-explain on their own.[51] Thus, to enable our students to self-explain we need to provide scaffolding. Asking students to annotate a worked example or their solution to a problem is one way, while another is to provide prompts when they are faced with worked examples. For example, you could share the incorrect worked example in Figure 2.5 with the students, whereby the prompts used to encourage students to self-explain are:

♦ What did Helaina do wrong in her first step?

♦ Would it have been okay to write $5 + 2 - 4x$? Explain why or why not.

The first prompt focuses on identifying the error – what did Helaina do wrong? Pair these types of prompts (often beginning with *what*: what is wrong? What mistake was made? What is the correct solution?) with those that encourage the students to elaborate and explain their reasoning – explain why or why not is used here. Prompts beginning with *why* help them to do this: why did Helaina rewrite the expression in this way? Figure 2.22 lists some example self-explanation prompts including my favourite, 'Give Helaina some advice so that she doesn't make this mistake again.'

---

1   What did [student name] do wrong?

2   Why did [student name] ...?

3   How did [student name] know to ...?

4   What can you change to make [student name]'s solution correct?

5   Would it have been okay to ...? Explain your reasoning.

6   Why didn't [student name] ... ?

7   If [student name] did ..., would they still get the correct solution?

8   Would it be okay to ... ? Explain your reasoning.

9   What does the ... stand for?

10 Why would ... have been an incorrect solution?

---

11 Would [student name] get the same solution if they … first? Explain your reasoning.

12 Give [student name] some advice so that she/he doesn't make this mistake again.

Figure 2.22. Examples of self-explanation prompts © SERP Institute[52]

Note that student self-explanation prompts can be used with every type of worked example, including correct worked examples. It is best to get the students to write down their responses – the key to this strategy is to self-explain, not explain to a peer or teacher. The excellent AlgebraByExample materials harness the combined power of worked examples and student self-explanation.

13. Consistency is Key

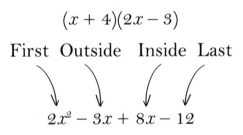

$$(x + 4)(2x - 3)$$

First Outside   Inside Last

$$2x^2 - 3x + 8x - 12$$

Figure 2.23. FOIL (first, outside, inside, last)

In the past I have fallen foul of teaching my students shortcuts or tricks. We share these, often having been taught them ourselves, in an effort to help our students remember procedures. A common example is FOIL (first, outer/outside, inner/inside, last). FOIL is used to help students remember how to expand the product of two binomials. The problem is that it is very easy for FOIL to fail. Consider the expansion of $(x + 2)(x + y + 3)$. Students taught FOIL would fail; students taught for understanding – by applying the distributive law – would not. We must avoid teaching our students shortcuts that *replace* understanding, especially those that work for only a narrow range of problems.

It is not just shortcuts that can cause problems for our students. Sometimes methods that work in the moment seem seductive, yet they break under pressure – for example, using function machines to solve linear equations.

This method works well when a problem has an unknown on one side but fails when applied to problems with unknowns on both sides.

Naveen Rizvi, a maths teacher and blogger, uses this principle to ensure consistency in the methods she selects: "teaching methods for future learning should never contradict the teaching methods used for prior learning".[53] We must ensure that we teach our students methods that will work consistently across the broadest range of problems, without undermining what will follow.

In conclusion, the strategies in this chapter can be used to render your explanations bulletproof, which will put your students on the path to success.

Reflective questions

♦ Which strategies will have the most powerful impact on your teaching?

♦ How do you check the prior knowledge of the students you teach?

♦ How will you use worked examples to lower cognitive load?

♦ When planning to introduce a new concept, which examples of the concept and examples that are not the concept (non-concept) will you use to best convey the idea and avoid students creating mis-rules?

♦ How will you reflect upon how much talk is necessary to explain a new concept?

♦ How do your students respond to silent modelling?

♦ Do you consistently model exemplary use of mathematical language? How do you embed the expectation that your students will follow?

♦ What is the most appropriate strategy to bridge the concrete to abstract for the topic you are teaching?

♦ What additional/alternative representations are most effective for this topic?

♦ Are there manipulatives that would aid students' understanding of this topic? What is the clear rationale for their use?

♦ How do you make use of gesture in your teaching?

♦ How do you explicitly plan to use analogy in your teaching?

♦ Which strategies will be most powerful to enhance your explanation of a particular topic?

♦ How can you gain confidence to live model on the whiteboard instead of relying on prepared slides?

♦ Is the method you have selected to teach a topic applicable to the broadest possible range of problems, and are you avoiding shortcuts that replace understanding?

Endnotes

1 Shepard Barbash, *Clear Teaching: With Direct Instruction* (Arlington, VA: Education Consumers Foundation, 2012), p. 16.

2 Dylan Wiliam, *Embedded Formative Assessment* (Bloomington, IN: Solution Tree Press, 2011), p. 53.

3 Harry Fletcher-Wood, Ben Bignall, Lucy Blewett, Jen Calvert, Josh Goodrich and Emma McCrea, *The Learning Curriculum* (London: Institute for Teaching, 2018). Available at: https://khsbpp.files.wordpress.com/2018/06/ift-learning-curriculum-v1-2.pdf, p. 6.

4 Sal Khan does a great job of explaining the importance of prior knowledge: Let's Teach Mastery – Not Test Scores, *TED.com* [video] (2015). Available at: https://www.ted.com/talks/sal_khan_let_s_teach_for_mastery_not_test_scores?language=en#t-279632.

5 It is suggested that we lose the content of our working memory after about 30 seconds of inactivity and we can only hold between four to seven pieces of information at any one time: Kirschner et al., Why Minimal Guidance During Instruction Does Not Work.

6 Deans for Impact, *The Science of Learning* (Austin, TX: Deans for Impact, 2015). Available at: https://deansforimpact.org/wp-content/uploads/2016/12/The_Science_of_Learning.pdf, p. 3.

7 Centre for Education Statistics and Evaluation, *Cognitive Load Theory in Practice: Examples for the Classroom* (Sydney: CESE, 2018). Available at: https://www.cese.nsw.gov.au/images/stories/PDF/Cognitive_load_theory_practice_guide_AA.pdf, p. 1.

8 See https://twitter.com/dylanwiliam/status/824682504602943489?lang=en.

9 Daisy Christodoulou, *Making Good Progress? The Future of Assessment for Learning* (Oxford: Oxford University Press, 2017), p. 67.

10 Find out more via Craig Barton's podcast: Kris Boulton – Part 1: Planning Lessons, Engelmann and Differentiation, *Mr Barton Maths Podcast* [audio] (17 July 2017). Available at: http://www.mrbartonmaths.com/blog/kris-boulton-part-1-planning-lessons-engelmann-and-differentiation/; or Kris' blog: My Best Planning – Part 1, … *To the Real* (12 August 2017). Available at: https://tothereal.wordpress.com/2017/08/12/my-best-planning-part-1/.

11 Centre for Education Statistics and Evaluation, *Cognitive Load Theory in Practice*, p. 11.

12 Sweller et al., *Cognitive Load Theory*, p. 107.

13 Sweller et al., *Cognitive Load Theory*.

14 In Sweller et al.'s *Cognitive Load Theory* this is referred to as the 'guidance fading effect'.

15 See Robert K. Atkinson, Alexander Renkl and Mary M. Merrill, Transitioning from Studying Examples to Solving Problems: Effects of Self-Explanation Prompts and Fading Worked-Out Steps, *Journal of Educational Psychology* 95(4) (2003): 774–783. Available at: https://www.researchgate.net/publication/200772684_Transitioning_From_Studying_Examples_to_Solving_Problems_Effects_of_Self-Explanation_Prompts_and_Fading_Worked-Out_Steps.

16 *Source*: Excerpt from AlgebraByExample used with permission of SERP © Strategic Education Research Partnership serpinstitute.org. AlgebraByExample provides an amazing bank of correct and incorrect worked examples pairs: http://math.serpmedia.org/algebra_by_example/.

17 See Kelly M. McGinn, Karin E. Lange and Julie L. Booth, A Worked Example for Creating Worked Examples, *Mathematics Teaching in the Middle School* 21(1) (2015): 27–33. Available at: https://www.montana.edu/em/direction/MTMS_2015_CreatingWorkedExamples.pdf.

18 More misconceptions can be explored at Michael Pershan's website: http://mathmistakes.org or at http://www.calculatorsoftware.co.uk/classicmistake/gallery.htm.

19 See https://math.serpmedia.org/algebra_by_example/download_center.html.

20 *Source*: Excerpt from AlgebraByExample used with permission of SERP © Strategic Education Research Partnership serpinstitute.org.

21 Institute of Education Sciences, *Teaching Strategies for Improving Algebra Knowledge in Middle and High School Students* (Washington, DC: IES, 2015). Available at: https://ies.ed.gov/ncee/wwc/Docs/PracticeGuide/wwc_algebra_040715.pdf, p. 26.

22 We examine applications of variation theory to practice in Chapter 3.

23 Angelika Kullberg, Ulla Runesson Kempe and Ference Marton, What Is Made Possible to Learn When Using the Variation Theory of Learning in Teaching Mathematics? *International Journal on Mathematics Education* 49 (2017): 559–569. Available at: https://link.springer.com/content/pdf/10.1007%2Fs11858-017-0858-4.pdf.

24 According to Jane Jones, former HMI national lead for mathematics: see Craig Barton, Jane Jones: Ofsted, Observations, Marking, Reasoning, *Mr Barton Maths Podcast* [audio] (3 January 2018). Available at: http://www.mrbartonmaths.com/blog/jane-jones-ofsted-observations-marking-reasoning/.

25 The relevant concept is fractions. Finding a non-concept for fractions makes sense.

26 National Centre for Excellence in the Teaching of Mathematics, *Mathematics Matters: Final Report* (Sheffield: NCETM, 2008). Available at: https://www.ncetm.org.uk/public/files/309231/Mathematics+Matters+Final+Report.pdf, p. 4.

27 Dani Quinn, Never Let Me Go, *Until I Know Better* (31 May 2017). Available at: https://missquinnmaths.wordpress.com/2017/05/31/never-let-me-go/.

28 Rachel Marks is a principal lecturer in mathematics education (primary) at the University of Brighton.

29 See Institute of Education Sciences, Teaching Strategies for Improving Algebra Knowledge in Middle and High School Students: Practice Guide Summary (2015). Available at: https://ies.ed.gov/ncee/wwc/Docs/practiceguide/wwc_algebra_summary_072115.pdf, p. 4.

30 *Source*: Adapted from Elizabeth M. Hughes, Sarah R. Powell and Elizabeth A. Stevens, Supporting Clear and Concise Mathematical Language, *Teaching Exceptional Children* 49(1) (2016): 7–17; Institute of Education Sciences, *Teaching Strategies for Improving Algebra Knowledge in Middle and High School Students* (Washington, DC: IES, 2015). Available at: https://ies.ed.gov/ncee/wwc/Docs/PracticeGuide/wwc_algebra_040715.pdf; and Karen S. Karp, Sarah B. Bush and Barbara J. Dougherty, 13 Rules That Expire, *Teaching Children Mathematics* 21(1) (2014): 18–25.

31 Courtesy of Bernard Murphy, programme lead at Mathematics in Education and Industry.

32 Jeremy Hodgen, Colin Foster and Dietmar Kuchemann, *Improving Mathematics in Key Stages Two and Three: Guidance Report* (London: Education Endowment Foundation, 2018). Available at: https://educationendowmentfoundation.org.uk/tools/guidance-reports/maths-ks-two-three/, p. 32. Using manipulatives and representations, which are more common in primary classrooms, is one of the eight recommendations made in the report.

33 Hodgen et al., *Improving Mathematics in Key Stages Two and Three: Guidance Report*, p. 10.

34 See http://mathsbot.com/#Manipulatives.

35 Courtesy of Adrian via Bruno Reddy's blog: Guest Blog: Circle Theorems and Hula Hoops, *Mr Reddy Maths Blog* (10 December 2012). Available at: http://mrreddy.com/blog/2012/12/guest-blog-circle-theorems-and-hula-hoops/.

36 An unknown side length is in itself an abstract concept – clearly we could measure the side length.

37 For more on algebra tiles see Mark McCourt, An Introduction to Algebra Tiles for Teaching Mathematics, *The Emaths Blog* (18 March 2018). Available at: https://markmccourt.blogspot.com/2018/03/an-introduction-to-algebra-tiles-for.html; and William Emeny, Algebra Tiles – From Counting to Completing the Square, *Great Maths Teaching Ideas* (4 April 2015). Available at: http://www.greatmathsteachingideas.com/2015/04/04/algebra-tiles-from-counting-to-completing-the-square/.

38 Henderson et al., *Improving Mathematics in Key Stages Two and Three: Evidence Review*.

39 See National Centre for Excellence in the Teaching of Mathematics, *Mathematics Glossary for Teachers in Key Stages 1 to 3* (January 2014). Available at: https://www.ncetm.org.uk/files/19226855/National+Curriculum+Glossary.pdf, p. 75.

40 See John Woodward, Sybilla Beckmann, Mark Driscoll, Megan Franke, Patricia Herzig, Asha Jitendra, Kenneth R. Koedinger and Philip Ogbuehi, *Improving Mathematical Problem Solving in Grades 4 Through 8*. IES Practice Guide. NCEE 2012-4055 (Washington, DC: Institute of Education Sciences, 2012).

41 *Source*: Malcolm Swan, *Standards Unit: Improving Learning in Mathematics: Challenges and Strategies* (London: Department for Education and Skills, 2005). Available at: https://spiremaths.co.uk/ilim/.

42 William Emeny has written an excellent blog about the scope of topics that lend themselves to bar models: Bar Modelling – A Powerful Visual Approach for Introducing Number Topics, *Great Maths Teaching Ideas* (26 December 2014). Available at: http://www.greatmathsteachingideas.com/2014/12/26/bar-modelling-a-powerful-visual-approach-for-introducing-number-topics/.

43 Jonathan Hall's bar model tool is great for this: http://mathsbot.com/manipulatives/bar.

44 See this zoomable number line: https://www.mathsisfun.com/numbers/number-line-zoom.html.

45 Henderson et al., *Improving Mathematics in Key Stages Two and Three: Evidence Review*.

46 David Wees has built one using GeoGebra: see https://www.geogebra.org/m/EQRR72ru.

47 Elizabeth Wakefield, Miriam A. Novack, Eliza L. Congdon, Steven Franconeri and Susan Goldin-Meadow, Gesture Helps Learners Learn, But Not Merely By Guiding Their Visual Attention, *Developmental Science* 21(6) (2018): e12664. Available at: http://visualthinking.psych.northwestern.edu/publications/WakefieldGesture2018.pdf.

48 Susan W. Cook, Ryan G. Duffy and Kimberly M. Fenn, Consolidation and Transfer of Learning After Observing Hand Gesture, *Child Development* 84(6) (2013): 1863–1871. Available at: https://pdfs.semanticscholar.org/a606/ca16285d30ceb9aa6be15380efb0dcf0e7c6.pdf.

49 For more on this see Daniel Willingham, Is It True That Some People Just Can't Do Math? I highly recommend it.

50 See yet another of Willingham's papers: Do Manipulatives Help Students Learn?, *American Educator* (Fall 2017): 25–40. Available at: https://www.aft.org/sites/default/files/periodicals/ae_fall2017_willingham.pdf.

51 Kelsey Gilbert, Self-Explanation as a Study Strategy for Math, *The Learning Scientists* (12 July 2016). Available at: http://www.learningscientists.org/blog/2016/7/12-1.

52 *Source*: Excerpt from AlgebraByExample used with permission of SERP © Strategic Education Research Partnership serpinstitute.org.

53 Naveen Rizvi, Engelmann Insights: Structuring Teaching for the Weakest Pupils (Part 1), *Conception of the Good* (11 March 2018). Available at: http://conceptionofthegood.co.uk/?p=569.

Chapter 3

Practice

Practice doesn't make perfect, *practice makes permanent.*[1]

When we talk about practice we mean doing something regularly in order to become better at it. In the same way that you cannot learn to play the guitar without practice, you cannot master solving equations without practice. If done effectively, practice can pave the pathway to expertise. Unfortunately this takes time.

Luckily, the science of expertise has uncovered something that's as important as the amount of practice – and that we are more able to leverage in the classroom. Anders Ericsson, the internationally renowned researcher into expertise, suggests that the type of practice is as important as the amount.[2] And, even more interesting, that expert performance is the result of *deliberate practice*, rather than just innate talent. This means that if we are able to offer more effective practice opportunities for all students, we may be able to accelerate every one of them on a journey towards mastery.

Deliberate practice is purposeful, systematic and focused intently on improving performance. It is the result of rigorous instructional design and precise actionable feedback. It differs from normal practice, which is characterised by mindless repetition, and in a classroom context might be categorised as 'more of the same'.

While Ericsson himself suggests that deliberate practice is not easily replicable in the classroom setting,[3] there are features of this type of practice that we can leverage:

♦ Use carefully crafted practice tasks so that practice is expert led and focused.

♦ Isolate the skill we want students to practise so they are working towards well-defined, specific goals that are crafted in a carefully chosen order.

♦ Provide immediate feedback so that students are quickly able to check and adjust accordingly.

These elements are addressed across the book: we discussed isolating the skill in Chapter 2, we will consider immediate feedback in Chapter 5 and in this chapter we look specifically at expert task design.

Our goal with practice is for students to achieve fluency by maximising *depth* and *longevity*, so they are able to calculate *accurately* (find correct solutions), *efficiently* (using an appropriate strategy or algorithm with speed) and *flexibly* (adapting strategy and transferring across contexts). By depth, we mean that students move beyond procedures, building conceptual understanding and making links and connections across mathematical topics. If we can enable them to do this, they will be better able to reason and solve problems. By maximising longevity, we ensure that learning is long-lasting.

There is an interesting and useful by-product of deep understanding: we remember things that we understand for longer. This is because we create more cues. When we retrieve information from our long-term memory we use cues or pathways. The more cues we have for the information, the more likely it is that we are able to retrieve information over time. For example, rather than just knowing the formula for the area of a circle, a student might understand why the area is given by πr^2 (see Figure 3.1), the hope being that the depth of their understanding is strengthened as a result of exposure to these representations.

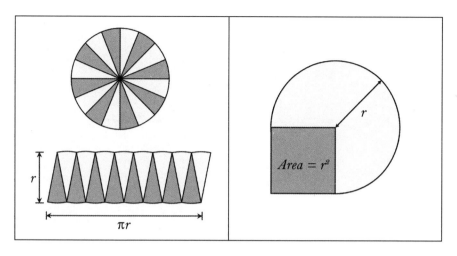

Figure 3.1. Images to support deeper understanding
of why the area of a circle is given by πr^2 [4]

We have all experienced that sinking feeling when we mark a test, only to discover that the students seem to have forgotten much of what we have taught them over the previous term or year. This is due to a feature of the memory called interference, which is the process of forgetting that occurs naturally over the passage of time. When Ebbinghaus studied interference back in 1885, his results led to the creation of the forgetting curve, which gives us a stark visual reminder of why students forget what they have been taught.[5] Our brains are programmed to forget; it's neither our nor our students' fault.

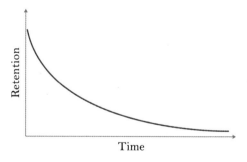

Figure 3.2. Ebbinghaus' forgetting curve[6]

The good news is that we are able to overcome the impact of interference by exploiting practice design. We can create learning experiences with outcomes that are more durable so the information remains available to our students for longer.

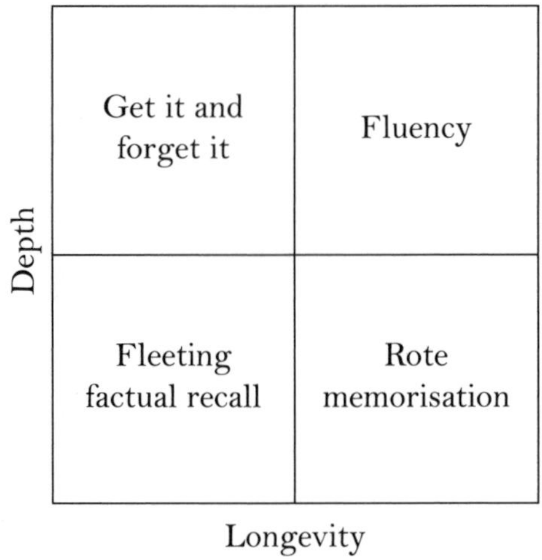

Figure 3.3. Impact of longevity and depth on fluency[7]

If we can offer our students practice that explicitly builds both depth and longevity, we will also begin to build fluency (Figure 3.3). This means they are less prone to forgetting and better able to transfer and apply knowledge to unfamiliar problems. What more could we want!

The strategies in this chapter do just that – build depth and longevity.

Purpose	Strategies
Depth	1 Procedural Variation 2 Fluency Synthesis 3 Goal-Free Problems 4 Swan's Top Tasks 5 Look Before You Leap
Longevity	6 Retrieval Practice 7 Spaced Practice 8 Interleaved Practice

Strategies for Depth of Understanding

One feature of deliberate practice is the use of expertly crafted tasks. What we mean here by task is a set of problems to practise. What follows are strategies that help us create these expertly crafted tasks.

1. Procedural Variation

We first met variation as a powerful condition for focusing student attention in strategy 3 in Chapter 2. Likewise, we can harness the power of variation and the principles of sameness and difference in the practice that our students do.

Consider the set of problems shown in Figure 3.4. Imagine a teacher wants their students to practise finding the gradient of a straight line between two points. They could set the following set of problems. Take a moment to do them yourself.

Find the gradient between each of the following pairs of points:

(4, 3) and (8, 12)	(-2, -1) and (-10, 1)
(7, 4) and (-4, 8)	(8, -7) and (11, -1)
(6, -4) and (6, 7)	(-5, 2) and (10, 6)
(-5, 2) and (-3, -9)	(-6, -9) and (-6, -8)

Figure 3.4. Normal practice[8]

This would be considered *normal practice* as seen in many textbooks. The problems increase in perceived difficulty through the inclusion of negative numbers. However, they offer nothing more than mechanical practice. In fact, we could argue that the students are practising subtraction and division rather than developing an understanding of the concept of gradient. If we asked the students to represent these on one coordinate grid, they would be an incoherent jumble of irrelevant points and line segments. The late, great Professor Malcolm Swan went so far as to say that "if practice is just repeating the same procedure with different numbers, chosen randomly, then it has no purpose".[9]

Now take a look at the problems in Figure 3.5. Do them before reading on.

Find the gradient between each of the following pairs of points:

$(4, 3)$ and $(8, 12)$	$(4, 3)$ and $(4, 12)$
$(4, 3)$ and $(7, 12)$	$(4, 3)$ and $(3, 12)$
$(4, 3)$ and $(6, 12)$	$(4, 3)$ and $(2, 12)$
$(4, 3)$ and $(5, 12)$	$(4, 3)$ and $(1, 12)$

Figure 3.5. Procedural variation[10]

This more effective set of problems exemplifies how variation might be used to better focus student attention. At first glance, it appears that these problems are less useful, given that they are computationally easier (most of the coordinate pairs are the same and there are no negative numbers). Yet it is this subtle variation that draws student attention to the meaning of gradient, and therefore enables them to make progress towards understanding it. In this example, this is achieved by systematically varying one aspect, leaving everything else unchanged: one of the x coordinates is systematically varied, while all the others remain the same.

By doing this, student attention is focused on one significant aspect of a concept. They are led down a path whereby they are encouraged to make connections and see patterns. We can assist them on this journey by prompting them to explicitly seek these connections. Through this experience, they gain a deeper understanding of the concept of gradient (conceptual understanding), while also practising the skill of calculating gradients (procedural knowledge).

Note that in this instance, challenging students to plot these line segments on a coordinate grid can help them to further build on their understanding of gradient, assisting them in reaching the heart of the concept.

Tasks that apply variation in this way, such as those in Figures 3.5 and 3.6, are best tackled near the beginning of a learning episode and are particularly powerful for developing conceptual understanding through procedural knowledge.

1	$(c + 6)$
2	$(c + 6) + (c + 6)$
3	$(c + 6) + (c + 6) + (c + 6)$
4	$(c + 6) + (c + 6) + (c + 6) + (c + 6)$
5	$(c + 6) + (c + 6) + (c + 6) + (c + 6) + (c + 6)$
6	$(c + 6) + (c + 6) + (c + 6) + 2(c + 6)$
7	$3(c + 6) + 2(c + 6)$
8	$3(c + 6) + 2(6 + c)$
9	$3(6 + c) + 2(c + 6)$
10	$3(c - 6) + 2(c - 6)$
11	$3(c - 6) + (c - 6)$
12	$3(c - 6) - (c - 6)$

Figure 3.6. Example of a procedural variation problem set for knowing that brackets represent repeated addition. Students are tasked with simplifying where possible while keeping the brackets[11]

This strategy comes with a side of caution: the most important feature of procedural variation is prompting students to examine and reflect on the impact of the variation. It is through this process that they will begin to make connections, and it is in making these connections that they will start to gain a deeper, conceptual understanding. Without this reflection, students are merely doing sets of repetitive, boring and somewhat easy problems.

Prompts to use with students to ensure they attend to what is being varied and the consequences of that variation include:

♦ What is the same and what is different?

♦ What changes and what stays the same?

♦ What do you notice?

♦ Why might this be happening?

♦ What does it mean?

♦ What might come next?

Examples of similar procedural variation problem sets can be found at Craig Barton's https://variationtheory.com (this is often referred to as variation theory or intelligent practice), in *Deliberate Maths: Expertly Designed Practice Question Sets* – co-authored by Deb Friis and me – or you can make them yourself. They take a bit of time to create, but doing so is great professional development as contemplating how to use variation to focus student attention will help you to gain a deeper understanding of the concept you are attempting to teach and the impact the practice will have on your students. Remember, for this approach to variation, the key is to vary just one aspect while keeping everything else constant (invariant). Interestingly, whether we learn about what varies when other things are kept the same, or about what stays the same when other things vary, is up for debate.[12]

Note that with this strategy (and strategy 3, Concept/Non-concept, in Chapter 2) we are just scratching the surface of how we can use variation in our teaching to help our students attend to the relevant features of a concept. To dig deeper, read the Association of Teachers of Mathematics' variation in mathematics teaching and learning edited collection of writing.[13]

2. Fluency Synthesis

Fluency synthesis tasks require students to apply their knowledge to more challenging procedural problems. In doing so, it is anticipated that they will build fluency in two ways:

1   Through exposure to more challenging applications of a procedure so their procedural knowledge becomes more secure.

2   By revisiting important, high-tariff knowledge such as calculating with negative numbers, fractions and decimal numbers.

Analysing examples is probably the best way to get to grips with this strategy. Imagine we are planning a learning episode for calculating the area of a triangle. By the end of the episode, we want the students to be able to find the area of a triangle no matter what type of triangle and what units are used for the lengths. We also want them to be able to decide, when given too much information, which information is necessary and, equally, to know when not enough information has been given. Have a go at the set of problems in Figure 3.7.

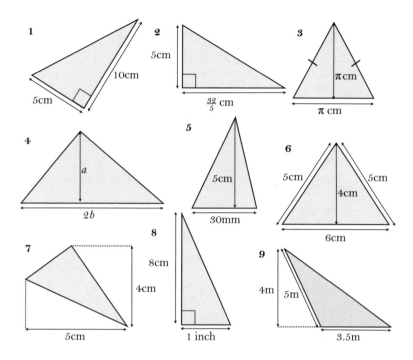

Figure 3.7. Examples of fluency synthesis problems for the area of a triangle

Fluency synthesis problems probe understanding as well as building fluency. Students would be unable to solve problems 6 and 9, or notice that they are not given the correct information to solve problem 7, without a deep understanding of how to calculate the area of a triangle.

A set of fluency synthesis problems are likely to:

♦ Require the regular retrieval of high-tariff knowledge such as negative numbers, fractions, decimals, zero, one, pi, unit conversions, surds and algebra (as in problems 2, 3, 4, 5 and 8).

♦ Present students with boundary cases (problems 1, 7 and 9).[14]

♦ Include problems with too little or too much information (problems 6, 7 and 9).

Figure 3.8 provides another example – a set of 10 problems on substitution (which uses $y = mx + c$ in preparation for working with straight line graphs at a later time). Take a moment to solve them yourself.

Calculate the value of y in the equation $y = 3x + 5$ given the following values for x:	
1 $x = 1$	6 $x = -0.5$
2 $x = \frac{1}{2}$	7 $x = -\sqrt{49}$
3 $x = \frac{5}{3}$	8 $x = \sqrt{2}$
4 $x = 0$	9 $x = f$
5 $x = -\frac{1}{3}$	10 $x = \pi$

Figure 3.8. Example of a problem set incorporating fluency synthesis for substitution[15]

Note that, depending on the topic, it is not always possible to include problems of every type. For example, it is not appropriate to use negative numbers when working with area, and it is very difficult to offer a problem with too much or too little information when working with substitution, although one might argue that problem 9 fulfils this.

For students to be successful with these tasks, they must possess a solid grounding in the high-tariff knowledge. Asking them to complete problems that assume knowledge of negative numbers when they have none, or if their knowledge is fragile, will lead to failure.

Fluency synthesis problem sets can be created by referring to the examples in Figures 3.7 and 3.8 and the bullet list on page 89. That said, don't feel that you need to create a whole set – adding one problem for each bullet point to your usual practice is a great starting point. Alternatively, you can find them in Friis and McCrea's *Deliberate Maths*. Dave Taylor, a maths teacher who creates and shares resources, has created Increasingly Difficult Questions (IDQs) which offer some of the characteristics of fluency synthesis.[16]

3. Goal-Free Problems

Solving unfamiliar problems can place a strain on working memory. This is particularly acute for novices (those with less knowledge and experience) as they tend to solve problems in an inefficient way. Most problems we come across have a goal or endpoint. When faced with an unfamiliar problem, novices tend to work backwards from the goal. This means that they consider all the different means or approaches by which they might be able to achieve their goal, while also keeping the goal in mind – and this can lead to cognitive overload.

This is when goal-free problems can help. The goal-free effect, drawn from Sweller's cognitive load theory, suggests, counterintuitively, that problems with a non-specific goal impose a lower cognitive load than those with a specific goal. For example, posing the problem in Figure 3.9 without offering any further information leaves the students free to explore the problem without having to keep in mind the goal, thereby lowering the cognitive load.

Deb wants to buy some fruit. She has £3 to spend. Bananas are 20p and apples are 15p.

Figure 3.9. Example of a goal-free problem

Goal-free problems are easy to create: remove the goal from the problem, leaving just the information and/or a diagram. For example, rather than asking the students to "find angle x", it might be better to ask them to "find the value of as many angles as possible".[17] Past exam papers provide a great resource for goal-free problems: remove the goal from the diagram, graph or table and task the students with working out whatever they can. If there is a diagram, encourage them to annotate it. Ask them to talk to a peer about what they have found. When you reveal the actual goal, it is very likely that they will be part way towards the solution and feel more confident that they can solve it than if they had been presented with the goal in the first place.

If used regularly, this can be a great strategy for students to use when they are stuck, particularly in an exam context. They can cover up the goal and try to figure out stuff in the hope that it will get them closer to the solution.

4. Swan's Top Tasks

Malcolm Swan led a project that sought to design better learning experiences to foster conceptual understanding. The outcomes of this project were twofold. Firstly, five task 'types' were proposed to inform the design of practice tasks. Secondly, a suite of materials, called the *Standards*

Unit: Improving Learning in Mathematics, were created that not only exemplified these task types for various topics but also described how they might be used with students – providing materials that are ripe for use as part of a learning episode. We can also use these five task types to create our own tasks.

The five task types are:[18]

---

1   *Classifying mathematical objects*

"Learners devise their own classifications for mathematical objects, and apply classifications devised by others. They learn to discriminate carefully and recognise the properties of objects. They also develop mathematical language and definitions."

For example, when teaching solving quadratic equations, I tasked students to devise their own classification flow chart to expose their decision-making processes about which method to use. Another example, in which students apply classifications that are provided to them, comes from the *Standards Unit* materials. Students are provided with cards with shapes on and challenged to classify them in a range of ways, two of which are shown.

	No parallel sides	Two parallel sides	Two pairs of parallel sides
No equal sides			
Two equal sides			
Two pairs of equal sides			

	Small area	Large area
Small perimeter		
Large perimeter		

Figure 3.10. Two-way classification tables[19]

2 Interpreting multiple representations

"Learners match cards showing different representations of the same mathematical idea. They draw links between different representations and develop new mental images for concepts."

This example tasks students to translate between symbols, words, tables and area representations of algebraic expressions.

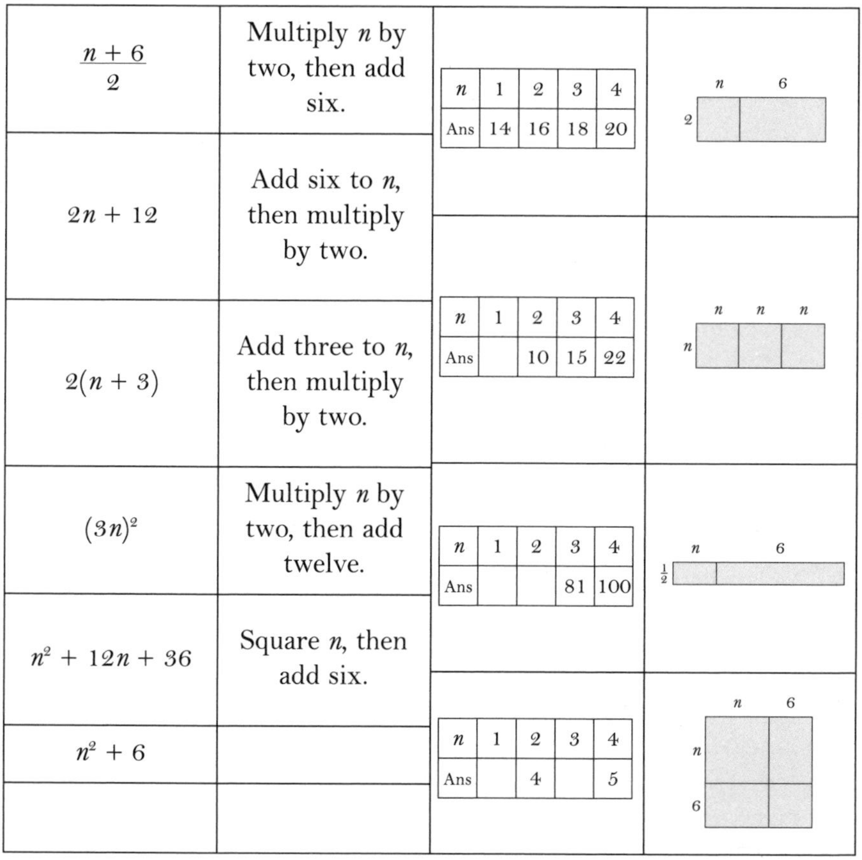

Figure 3.11. Matching multiple representations (blank cards are to be completed by the students)[20]

3 Evaluating mathematical statements

"Learners decide whether given statements are 'always true', 'sometimes true' or 'never true'. They are encouraged to develop rigorous mathematical arguments and justifications, and to devise examples and counterexamples to defend their reasoning."

For example, is the following statement always, sometimes or never true? If sometimes, then when? *Jim got a 15% pay rise. Jane got a 10% pay rise. So Jim's pay rise was greater than Jane's.*

4   **Creating problems**

"Learners devise their own problems or problem variants for other students to solve. This offers them the opportunity to be creative and 'own' problems. While others attempt to solve them, they take on the role of teacher and explainer. The 'doing' and 'undoing' processes of mathematics are vividly exemplified."

For example, one partner may create an equation, then the other tries to solve it.

5   **Analysing reasoning and solutions**

"Learners compare different methods for doing a problem, organise solutions and/or diagnose the causes of errors in solutions. They begin to recognise that there are alternative pathways through a problem, and develop their own chains of reasoning."

The Comparison Worked Example and Incorrect Worked Examples strategies in Chapter 2 offer great practical ways of getting students to "compare different methods for doing a problem" and "diagnose the causes of errors in solutions" respectively. Meanwhile, in the example in Figure 3.12, students are supported to develop chains of reasoning by being offered the steps on cards which they are required to sequence correctly. The focus of attention is therefore on the underlying logic and structure of the solution rather than its technical accuracy.

$y = x^3 - 4x^2 + 5x + 11$	$y = x^3 - x^2 - x + 5$	$(3x - 5)(x - 1) = 0$	$(3x + 1)(x - 1) = 0$
$y = x^3 - 7x^2 - 5x + 9$	$3x^2 - 8x + 5 = 0$	$x = 5, \frac{d^2y}{dx^2} = \dots$	$\frac{dy}{dx} = 3x^2 - 8x + 5$
$\frac{d^2y}{dx^2} = 6x - 8$	$\frac{dy}{dx} = 3x^2 - 14x - 5$	$x = -\frac{1}{3}, \frac{d^2y}{dx^2} = \dots$	$x = -\frac{1}{3}, x = 1$
$x = -\frac{1}{3}, \frac{d^2y}{dx^2} = \dots$	$x = \frac{5}{3}, x = 1$	$\frac{d^2y}{dx^2} = 6x - 14$	$x = \frac{5}{3}, \frac{d^2y}{dx^2} = \dots$
$\frac{dy}{dx} = 3x^2 - 2x - 1$	$\frac{d^2y}{dx^2} = 6x - 2$	Maximum is at …	Minimum is at …

$x = 1, \frac{d^2y}{dx^2} = \ldots$	$x = -\frac{1}{3}, x = 5$	Minimum is at …	Maximum is at …
$(3x + 1)(x - 5)$ $= 0$	$x = 1, \frac{d^2y}{dx^2} = \ldots$	Maximum is at …	Minimum is at …
$3x^2 - 14x - 5 = 0$	$3x^2 - 2x - 1 = 0$		

Figure 3.12. Ordering chains of reasoning[21]

5. Look Before You Leap

Have a go at the problem in Figure 3.13.

Four bags contain a large number of 1s, 3s, 5s and 7s.

Pick any 10 numbers from the bags above so that their total is 37.

Figure 3.13. Make 37[22]

How far did you get before you noticed?[23] This is one of my favourite problems to give to teachers to illustrate this strategy: often we don't stop and think before tackling a problem, and neither do our students. We need to encourage them to look before they leap. To do this we need to expose them to the types of problems that look complicated but are actually fairly straightforward.

Take this example:

$$6.5 \times 14.8 + 35 \times 1.48$$

One way to tackle this is to calculate 6.5×14.8, then calculate 35×1.48 and then add them together – a complex task. However, if we can build a culture whereby students take a moment to stop and think, they may just notice that with a slight tweak this problem is not as tricky as it first appears.[24] This is not an easy thing to train our students to do – they need exposure and practice. Here are some other examples:

$$\frac{17 + 17 + 17}{3}$$

$$9999 + 999 + 999 + 9$$

$\frac{17}{34}$ of 20

Which is larger $\frac{1}{98}$ or $\frac{1}{99}$?

Sum the numbers 1 to 100

$10 \div \frac{1}{2}$

Strategies for Longevity

To combat forgetting we need to introduce what are referred to as 'desirable difficulties'. These are strategies that make learning more difficult, but are desirable because they help to make the learning last – they offer longevity. Frustratingly, desirable difficulties will cause the students to appear to make less progress in the short term. However, there is increasing evidence that, over the long term, desirable difficulties – in the form of retrieval, spacing and interleaving – are powerful strategies for longevity. We will consider each of these below.

6. Retrieval Practice

When we teach our aim is to try to get information into the students' memories. It took me a long time to realise that getting the information back out again is just as important. Getting students to retrieve information is a vital part of the learning process and is key to improving longevity.

Retrieval practice is the process of withdrawing something that we have learned from long-term memory back into working memory. In doing so, we consolidate that learning, which makes it more retrievable later and improves memory and transfer.[25] It's nothing new – flashcards is an example that has been around for ages. What is new is the body of research which suggests that nothing cements long-term learning as powerfully as retrieval practice.[26]

There are many different ways to encourage students to retrieve information from their long-term memory. We can ask them to write down everything they know about a topic or one thing they learned in their last lesson, create concept maps for a topic, use flashcards, or describe and explain ideas from memory in pairs. Homework provides an excellent opportunity for retrieval practice, assuming that students do not have notes to which they can refer. Even school corridors provide opportunities for retrieval practice – I've been known to ask students their times tables as they pass me by!

Knowledge organisers are hugely popular and help to codify factual knowledge to support retrieval practice. However, my attempts to replicate this success in maths have proved futile. For example, when trying to create a knowledge organiser for solving linear equations, I struggled to identify the knowledge associated with it that could easily be explained in words. Over time, I came to the conclusion that knowledge organisers just don't work as well for maths. Thankfully, Kris Boulton has helped me to clarify my thinking on why: knowledge organisers organise facts rather than knowledge, of which maths has very little. There are lots of processes and concepts but very few facts. Thus, knowledge organisers aren't well suited to maths. That said, lots of schools are using them to support the recall of vocabulary, particularly subject-specific vocabulary. In this respect, they are likely to be a useful tool for retrieval and self-quizzing of maths vocabulary.

Low-Stakes Testing

The best way to induce retrieval is through testing – testing *for* learning. This feels incredibly counterintuitive, especially given the current climate where there is a sense that our students are already over-tested. Consider the following question and commit to a solution before you read on.

Which of these study patterns is more likely to result in long-term learning?

1   Study study study study – test

2   Study study study test – test

3   Study study test test – test

4   Study test test test – test

Most of us will pick 1. It just feels right, doesn't it? Spaced repetitions of study are bound to result in better results, right? Wrong. The most successful pattern is in fact 4. Having just one study session, followed by three short testing sessions, and then a final assessment, outperforms any other pattern.[27] And, as an added bonus, there is evidence to suggest that testing can improve transfer of knowledge to new contexts.[28]

These aren't just any old tests. They need to be regular low-stakes tests – it is probably better to refer to them as quizzes. Regular means weekly or, at worst, fortnightly. Make them low stakes by getting the students to mark their own work and not collecting in the marks. This strategy works because of the retrieval that occurs during the test – the marks themselves are irrelevant. Don't be swayed into further reducing the stakes by making the test open book. If the students are able to access their notes, they are not doing the required retrieval.

Allowing students to mark their own tests gives us another fascinating benefit due to the hypercorrection effect. When we find out that something we thought was correct is, in fact, incorrect, we are less likely to make the same mistake again. The more confident the students are that they are correct, the more this effect is boosted. It might also be worth getting them to add a confidence rating to each problem – analysing incorrect answers with a higher confidence rating will have even more power.

My initial reaction was that weekly testing would increase anxiety in my students. However, research suggests that the opposite is true – that frequent low-stakes or no-stakes tests in the classroom actually help to reduce test anxiety.[29] It is likely due to students feeling better practised and better prepared for higher stakes end-of-year and formal exams. A final note: always tell your students when they have a quiz coming up. The evidence suggests that they will perform better as a result.[30]

Efrat Furst likens this process to climbing: "Learning by testing is like choosing to climb the higher peak: it takes more will, effort, and sweat, but what you gain, you will not forget."[31]

7. Spaced Practice

The first time we learn something it is like drawing a shape in the sand on a beach. At the time it is crystal clear, but it soon fades when the tide comes in and washes over it, leaving only a faint imprint. Yet the more we return over time to redraw this shape, the more resilient it will become to the blurring effects of the tide. Likewise, the more we return to something we have previously learned, the more resilient it will become to the effects of forgetting.

Spacing is a powerful strategy that boosts learning by spreading lessons and retrieval opportunities over time so learning is not crammed in all at once. By returning to content every so often, the students' knowledge has had time to rest and be refreshed.[32]

Retrieval practice is spacing's best friend – take all of the strategies that induce retrieval and space them out. For example, having taught a learning episode on probability, revisit it several times over the following days, weeks and months through starters, homeworks and quizzes. Rather than give a homework straight after teaching a topic, delay it until a week later. Postpone your test for the learning episode until two or three weeks after you have taught it. Figure 3.14 shows what happens to Ebbinghaus' forgetting curve when we space our retrieval out over time.

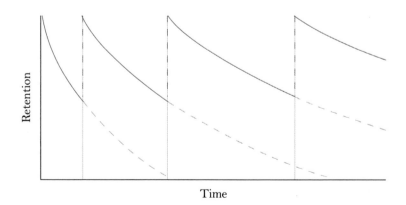

Figure 3.14. Ebbinghaus' forgetting curve with spaced retrieval practice

Notice that the gaps between retrievals increase over time – we need to redraw our shape in the sand less and less frequently as time goes on. Unfortunately, we don't yet know what the optimum spacings are because this will vary based on student and topic.

Fluency synthesis tasks (strategy 2) demonstrate spacing at work. Due to the inclusion of negative numbers, fractions, decimal numbers and so on, tasks using fluency synthesis force regular retrieval of important numeracy skills over time.

8. Interleaved Practice

When students practise during the lesson, they generally practise the topic we have just taught. If we are teaching trigonometry, they practise the application of trigonometry. While this seems logical, it means that students fail to practise the hardest part of solving problems – how to start. In a lesson on trigonometry, the students know that to solve any given problem, they need to apply trigonometry. The first and most difficult step of the problem has been removed – identifying that trigonometry is needed to solve it.

A problem that requires trigonometry outside of a lesson on trigonometry is far more challenging. What the students might recognise first is a triangle, meaning that it could be a problem about area, perimeter, angles, similarity, Pythagoras' theorem or trigonometry. Narrowing this down is a complex task.

Yet the GCSE maths exams, and indeed most student assessments, require students to do this – they are interleaved. Every problem requires the retrieval of different knowledge – for example, first there is a problem requiring fractions to decimal number conversions, next a perimeter problem, then a proportion problem and so on. In this sense, interleaved practice is commonplace in assessment but less so in our teaching – which is a problem. We need to give our students more exposure to interleaved practice in order for them to succeed in exams. Craig Barton's SSDD problems are an excellent place to start.[33]

One way to ensure that students gain explicit practice in identifying which strategy they need to use to solve a particular problem is to provide them with interleaved problems and ask them to complete the first step or first line of working only. In this way, they get more practice at identifying the topic *and* the strategy. Past exam papers are a good resource for this.

There is another incredibly interesting aspect of interleaving: *contextual interference*. Imagine the students are completing some trigonometry practice within the confines of a trigonometry lesson. To their surprise, when they get to the fifth problem, they find that it does not require trigonometry to solve it; instead, it requires them to find the product of two decimal numbers. They do so and continue to the next problem which takes them back to using trigonometry. Interrupting the students' thinking in this way is great for the longevity of learning.

To create sets of problems that cause contextual interference is easy. In a set of 10 problems, for example, you might make a couple about something other than what you are explicitly teaching (preferably something that you know the students need to practise). Figure 3.15 models this process.

---

1 If $a + b$ is 12, what is $a + b - 15$?

2 If $a + b$ is π, what is $a + b + 2$?

3 If $a + b$ is $\frac{1}{2}$, what is $a + b - \frac{1}{2}$?

4 If $a + b$ is 6, what is $a + b + c$?

5 Calculate $24 - 3 \times 2^3$.

6 If $a + b$ is 0, what is $a + b + c$?

7 If $a + b$ is c, what is $a + b + c$?

8 If $a + b$ is $2b$, what is a?

9 If $2(a + b)$ is 6, what is $4a + 4b$?

10 Sum the numbers 1 to 10.

11 If $a + b + c$ is 7, what is a?

12 If $a + b$ is 7, what is $a - b$?

Figure 3.15. Example set of interleaved problems on manipulating expressions. The fifth and tenth problem cause contextual interference[34]

A conflicting aspect of interleaving is that it slows down learning. Students will take longer to solve a set of problems if they are made to think about something else in the process. However, there is strong evidence that it makes learning last longer, which is obviously desirable.

We might think that there is a natural progression for interleaving to be implemented at a curriculum level, whereby several learning episodes are interleaved (see Figure 3.16). However, this approach is not recommended as there is as yet no evidence to suggest that it works. Furthermore, my sense is that the way in which our students experience the school day means that we could argue that we are already interleaving at this level. Students move from subject to subject, so if they are studying fractions in maths, for example, this is interleaved with atoms in science, learning to play softball in PE, using verbs in the past tense in French and so on.

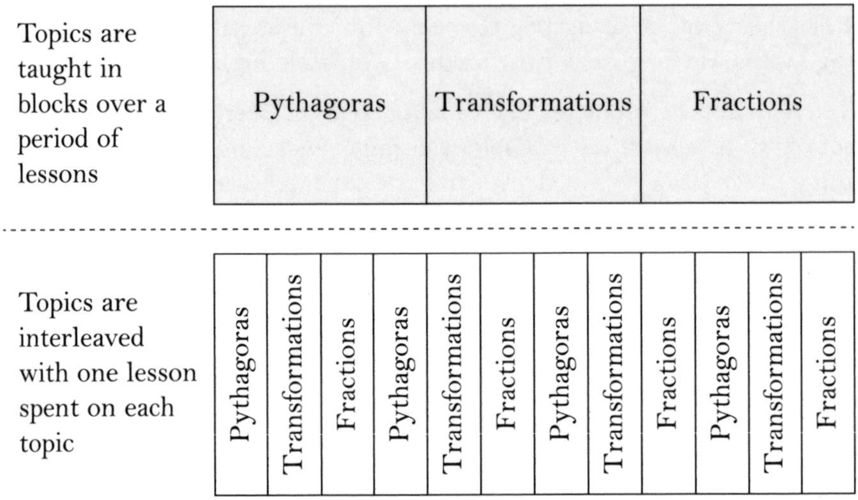

Topics are taught in blocks over a period of lessons	Pythagoras	Transformations	Fractions

Topics are interleaved with one lesson spent on each topic	Pythagoras	Transformations	Fractions	Pythagoras	Transformations	Fractions	Pythagoras	Transformations	Fractions	Pythagoras	Transformations	Fractions

Figure 3.16. Interleaving at a curriculum level

9. Nail the Numeracy

Quick retrieval of number facts is important for success in mathematics. It is likely that pupils who have problems retrieving addition, subtraction, multiplication, and division facts, including number bonds and multiples, will have difficulty understanding and using mathematical concepts they encounter later on in their studies.[35]

One of the biggest problems we face as maths teachers is our students' fragile factual knowledge and poor fluency. William Emeny, a teacher specialising in memory and curriculum design, embarked on a project to identify and map prior knowledge for GCSE maths. His findings were astounding but unsurprising: in his list of prior knowledge concepts by frequency, 16 of the top 20 were number. While we know that number is important, it has never been so clearly exposed.[36]

Some argue that students don't need to know their times tables – they contend that students can calculate 7 × 8 by doubling 7 × 2 twice, rather than storing it as factual knowledge. Knowing what we know about the limitations of working memory refutes this stance. If a student needs to calculate 67 × 48, there are several steps to the problem. If, in addition to those steps, the student also needs to calculate, rather than simply recall, 7 × 8 (and 6 × 8), they are likely to overload their working memory. This is why it is vital for students to acquire factual knowledge, including times tables. If a student can compute quickly with little effort, the burden on working memory is reduced.[37] Plus, it has been explicitly shown that knowledge of maths facts is associated with better performance on more complex maths tasks.[38]

We can help students to amass factual knowledge through regular, focused spaced retrieval practice, and there are some brilliant materials at our disposal. As a result of his network map project, Emeny created www. numeracyninjas.org, a free numeracy intervention designed to fill the gaps in students' basic mental calculation strategies. Times Tables Rock Stars (https://ttrockstars.com) is a carefully sequenced programme of daily times tables practice created by Bruno Reddy. Or you can create your own times table grid – remember that there are only 36 different single-digit multiplication facts. This is highlighted in Figure 3.17 where these facts are ordered in increasing difficulty as we move up the pyramid.

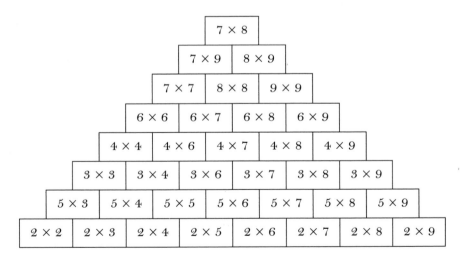

Figure 3.17. The pyramid of tables orders the 36 different single digit multiplication facts[39]

Vary which layer(s) of the pyramid you ask your students to practise completing – I find it useful to give them the top four rows more regularly.

10. Solve Problems

Returning to our understanding of the term problem solving (as discussed at the beginning of Chapter 1), it is useful to think of it as meaning solving unfamiliar problems – problems that our students have not yet met but have the knowledge to solve. They are sometimes referred to as non-standard, non-routine or word problems.

We need to challenge our students to solve unfamiliar problems as often as possible, ideally interleaved with our daily practice rather than during lessons dedicated to 'problem solving'. Problems presented to students need to be as unfamiliar as possible while staying within the students' realm of knowledge. If they are too far removed, they become inaccessible problems. For example, if I was asked to play an unfamiliar song on the guitar this would be an inaccessible problem for me because I wouldn't know the chords. But if I knew the chords, it would become an unfamiliar problem: I have the knowledge because I know the chords, I just haven't seen them arranged in that order before.

Research suggests that to support our students with solving unfamiliar problems, we should:

♦ Help them to make links with their prior knowledge:

◊ Give students hints to aid the retrieval of, and make connections to, something they have learned before.[40]

◊ Get students to compare familiar problems with the same mathematical structure but in different contexts in order to highlight exactly what they have in common (e.g. highlighting the proportionality aspect of equivalent fractions, similarity and pie charts).

♦ Share prompts (you can find some suggestions in strategy 6 in Chapter 4).

♦ Model how to solve unfamiliar problems (see strategy 6 in Chapter 4).

♦ Teach students to use representations (e.g. bar modelling in strategy 8, Chapter 2).

♦ Expose students to multiple strategies (e.g. the strategy comparison worked examples in strategy 2, Chapter 2).

Returning to our framework for practice (Figure 3.3), we have seen that is it through both depth and longevity that our students obtain fluency. Our task design strategies (strategies 1–5) all embed deep understanding. But no matter how deep our students' understanding, they are still likely to get it and forget it. It is only when we embed our strategies for longevity (strategies 6–10) that we have a shot at fluency.

Here are some final thoughts on practice that are useful to consider:

♦ *Use calculators.* The evidence suggests that primary students should not use calculators every day, but secondary students should have more frequent unrestricted access to them. Using a calculator does not generally harm a student's mental or·written calculation skills. In fact, studies have shown that using a calculator can have positive impacts, not only on mental calculation skills but also on problem solving and attitudes towards maths. Calculators should be integrated into the teaching of mental and other calculation approaches, and students should be taught to make considered decisions about when, where and why to use particular methods. The aim is to enable students to self-regulate their use of calculators, consequently making less (but better) use of them.[41]

♦ *Offer students both guided and independent practice.* At the start of a topic, practice needs to be more guided, with closer monitoring and more regular feedback. As time goes on, practice can become more independent.

♦ *Ensure students experience success so they are motivated to learn.* Rosenshine suggests that students should have a success rate of around 80%![42]

Remember: "It is virtually impossible to become proficient at a mental task without extended practice."[43]

Reflective questions

♦ Which strategies will have the most powerful impact on your teaching?

♦ How will you ensure that the students still know this next week, next month, next year?

♦ How do you provide the students with enough time to practise after explaining a new concept?

♦ Is the practice you get the students to do deliberate?

♦ Does the practice the students do fit with where they are in the learning episode?

♦ Are you building a culture in which the students think about problems before jumping in?

♦ Have you completed the practice that you want the students to do before the lesson?

♦ How are you building fluency?

♦ Are you using scaffolds to support practice and then removing them in a timely way to build independence?

♦ How are you ensuring the students are apply to able what they have been learning to unfamiliar problems?

Endnotes

1   No one is entirely sure who first coined this phrase. However, it appears in Doug Lemov, Erica Woolway and Katie Yezzi, *Practice Perfect: 42 Rules for Getting Better at Getting Better* (San Francisco, CA: Jossey-Bass, 2012), p. xii.

2   K. Anders Ericsson, Ralf T. Krampe and Clemens Tesch-Roemer, The Role of Deliberate Practice in the Acquisition of Expert Performance, *Psychological Review* 100(3) (1993): 363–406.

3   K. Anders Ericsson, Deliberate Practice Is What I Preach, *TES* (31 March 2017). Available at: https://www.tes.com/news/school-news/breaking-views/deliberate-practice-what-i-preach.

4   *Source*: The image on left is from https://goo.gl/GXhsde. The image on the right helps students to see that area of a circle must be less than $4r^2$. There is a wonderful GeoGebra applet to demonstrate the image on the left in action at: https://www.geogebra.org/m/fyqAUV22.

5   Despite Ebbinghaus' forgetting curve being the outcome of a study carried out in 1885, a 2015 study replicated his findings: Jaap M. J. Murre and Joeri Dros, Replication and Analysis of Ebbinghaus' Forgetting Curve, *PLOS ONE* 10(7) (2015): e0120644. Available at: https://doi.org/10.1371/journal.pone.0120644.

6   *Source*: https://www.inkling.com/blog/2015/08/why-google-changed-the-forgetting-curve/.

7   *Source*: Adapted from Peps Mccrea, *Memorable Teaching: Leveraging Memory to Build Deep and Durable Learning in the Classroom* (n.p.: CreateSpace), p. 14.

8   *Source*: Anne Watson and John Mason, Seeing an Exercise as a Single Mathematical Object: Using Variation to Structure Sense-Making, *Mathematical Thinking and Learning* 8(2) (2006): 91–111 at 109. Available at: http://oro.open.ac.uk/9764/1/06_MTL_Watson_%26_Mason.pdf.

9   See National Association of Mathematics Advisers, Five Myths of Mastery in Mathematics (December 2015). Available at: http://www.nama.org.uk/Downloads/Five%20Myths%20about%20Mathematics%20Mastery.pdf, p. 5.

10 *Source*: Watson and Mason, Seeing an Exercise as a Single Mathematical Object, at 109.

11 *Source*: Deb Friis and Emma McCrea, *Deliberate Maths: Expertly Designed Practice Question Sets* (in press).

12 See Anne Watson (ed.), *Variation in Mathematics Teaching and Learning. A Collection of Writing from ATM: Mathematics Teaching* (Derby: Association of Teachers of Mathematics, 2018).

13 Watson, *Variation in Mathematics Teaching and Learning.*

14 We explored these in strategy 3 in Chapter 2.

15 *Source:* Deb Friis and Emma McCrea, *Deliberate Maths: Expertly Designed Practice Question Sets* (in press).

16 See http://taylorda01.weebly.com/increasingly-difficult-questions.html.

17 See John Sweller, Story of a Research Program, in Sigmund Tobias, Dexter Fletcher and David Berliner (series eds), Acquired Wisdom Series. *Education Review* 23 (2016). Available at: http://dx.doi.org/10.14507/er.v23.2025, p. 4.

18 The following five task types are all from Malcolm Swan's *Collaborative Learning in Mathematics: A Challenge to Our Beliefs and Practices* (London: National Research and Development Centre/National Institute of Adult Continuing Education, 2006), pp. 143–150. The classroom materials can be found at http://spiremaths.co.uk/ilim with accompanying ActivInspire flipchart and SMART Notebook files.

19 *Source:* Standards Unit Task SS1 – Classifying shapes. Department for Education and Skills Further Education Standards Unit 2005. Available at: https://spiremaths.co.uk/wp-content/uploads/SS1.pdf.

20 *Source:* Standards Unit Task A1 – Interpreting algebraic expressions. Department for Education and Skills Further Education Standards Unit 2005. Available at: https://spiremaths.co.uk/wp-content/uploads/A1.pdf.

21 *Source:* Standards Unit Task C5 – Finding stationary points of cubic functions: Department for Education and Skills Further Education Standards Unit 2005. Available at: https://spiremaths.co.uk/wp-content/uploads/C5.pdf.

22 *Source:* Reproduced with permission of NRICH, University of Cambridge. Available at: http://nrich.maths.org/1885.

23 It is impossible for an even number of odd numbers to sum to an odd number.

24 By changing the calculation 6.5×14.8 to the equivalent calculation 65×1.48 we have $65 \times 1.48 + 35 \times 1.48$. 100×1.48 in total giving the solution 148.

25 See the retrieval practice concept map in Megan Smith, Yana Weinstein and Oliver Caviglioli, Concept Map: What Does Retrieval Practice Do?, *The Learning Scientists* (1 April 2016). Available at: http://www.learningscientists.org/blog/2016/4/1-1.

26 See Jennifer Gonzalez, Retrieval Practice: The Most Powerful Learning Strategy You're Not Using, *Cult of Pedagogy* (24 September 2017). Available at: https://www.cultofpedagogy.com/retrieval-practice/.

27 Henry L. Roediger III and Jeffrey D. Karpicke, Test-Enhanced Learning: Taking Memory Tests Improves Long-Term Retention, *Psychological Science* 17(3) (2006): 249–255. Available at: http://learninglab.psych.purdue.edu/downloads/2006_Roediger_Karpicke_PsychSci.pdf.

28 See Rebecca Allen, What If We Cannot Measure Pupil Progress?, *Musings on Education Policy* (23 May 2018). Available at: https://rebeccaallen.co.uk/2018/05/23/what-if-we-cannot-measure-pupil-progress/.

29 See Pooja Agarwal quoted in Megan Sumeracki, Retrieval Practice: Hiding Broccoli in the Brownies, *The Learning Scientists* (19 July 2018). Available at: http://www.learningscientists.org/blog/2018/7/19-1.

30 Michelle Rivers, How Test Expectancy Promotes Learning, *The Learning Scientists* (15 May 2018). Available at: http://www.learningscientists.org/blog/2018/5/15-1.

31 See https://sites.google.com/view/efratfurst/visuals?authuser=0.

32 See Pooja Agarwal on spacing at https://www.retrievalpractice.org/spacing.

33 SSDD stands for Same Surface, Different Deep – see https://ssddproblems.com.

34 *Source:* Deb Friis and Emma McCrea, *Deliberate Maths: Expertly Designed Practice Question Sets* (in press).

35 Hodgen et al., *Improving Mathematics in Key Stages Two and Three: Guidance Report*, p. 16.

36 See William Emeny, You've Never Seen the GCSE Maths Curriculum Like This Before ..., *Great Maths Teaching Ideas* (5 January 2014). Available at: http://www.greatmathsteachingideas. com/2014/01/05/youve-never-seen-the-gcse-maths-curriculum-like-this-before/.

37 See Bethany Rittle-Johnson and Nancy C. Jordan, *Synthesis of IES-Funded Research on Mathematics: 2002–2013*. NCER 2016-2003 (Washington, DC: Institute of Education Sciences 2016). Available at: https://ies.ed.gov/ncer/pubs/20162003/pdf/20162003.pdf.

38 See Willingham, Is It True That Some People Just Can't Do Math?

39 *Source*: http://thechalkface.net/resources/pyramid_of_tables.pdf.

40 See National Academies of Sciences, Engineering, and Medicine, *How People Learn II: Learners, Contexts, and Cultures* (Washington, DC: National Academies Press, 2018). Available at: https://doi.org/10.17226/24783.

41 See Henderson et al., *Improving Mathematics in Key Stages Two and Three: Evidence Review*, p. 88.

42 Barak Rosenshine, Principles of Instruction: Research-Based Strategies That All Teachers Should Know, *American Educator* (Spring 2012): 12–39. Available at: https://www.aft.org/sites/default/files/periodicals/Rosenshine.pdf.

43 Willingham, *Why Don't Students Like School?*, p. 149.

Chapter 4

Questioning

[Effective teachers] ask a large number of questions and check the responses of all students: Questions help students practice new information and connect new material to their prior learning.[1]

Teachers ask lots of questions – by one estimate, as many as 400 a day.[2] That is a lot of questions. And rightly so. Effective questioning is key to overcoming a cognitive bias we unknowingly suffer from called the 'curse of knowledge'. This well-documented bias centres around the idea that experts struggle to empathise with novices. It prevents us from being able to put ourselves in the position of our learners, and therefore we fail to fully understand what it means to be a novice. A subconscious narrative exists that if we understand it, then it must be easy to learn. Essentially, the curse of knowledge leads us to assume that the content we are teaching is more easily accessible than it actually is (see Figure 4.1).

A cleverly designed yet simple experiment provides an easy way to experience the curse of knowledge first hand – I urge you to give it a try. One person taps out a well-known song on a table while another person listens and tries to guess the song. When this experiment was carried out as part of a study, the 'tappers' predicted that the listeners would guess correctly half of the time. The listeners were able to identify the song just 2.5% of the time. The tappers were incredulous that the listeners were so poor at guessing. They had been cursed by their knowledge of the song. They failed to understand why the listeners couldn't guess correctly because they couldn't 'unknow' the song once they had it in their heads.[3] Being the listener is harder than it sounds.

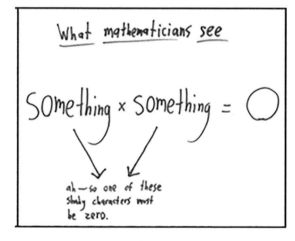

Figure 4.1. The curse of knowledge applied to the zero product property[4]

Students can also suffer from a cognitive bias called the Dunning–Kruger effect. It describes how novices can lack the understanding required to be able to correctly assess whether they understand or not. This means that some of our students may think they understand but are unable to accurately make that judgement. They don't understand but think they do: "Most learners cannot accurately judge what they do and don't know, and typically overestimate how well they have mastered material when they are finished studying."[5]

If we further consider that these two biases may be in operation at the same time, it is easy to imagine the havoc this might wreak in the classroom. The combination of teachers with the curse of knowledge and students experiencing the Dunning–Kruger effect can lead to the dangerous situation whereby both the teacher and the students believe they have grasped a concept when they have not. To overcome these biases, we need to get feedback from all students through effective questioning.

This chapter offers strategies to overcome both the curse of knowledge and the Dunning–Kruger effect. But before we think about how, let's consider why.

We ask questions for two reasons:

1   To focus student attention:

   ♦ To make connections and elaborate on ideas that they are likely to be unfamiliar with (e.g. Why can't we simplify $4x + 1$?)

   ♦ To consolidate through retrieval by asking closed questions (those with one clear answer) about familiar problems (e.g. What is the square root of 49?)

2   To gain feedback: information about what students know and don't know so that we can respond accordingly. This is where questioning links closely to feedback.

In order to focus attention and gain insightful feedback about student understanding, these questions must be well crafted and discerning – questions that make students think, that check and probe understanding and expose misconceptions.

Three aspects of questioning are important. The first is the purpose of the question – is it to focus attention through elaboration or retrieval or to gain information? Secondly, the design of our questions – that is, the content of our questions or what we ask. Lastly, the structures we put in place to build a culture that ensures a high quality of response and engagement from all of our students. Even the most exquisitely designed questions fail if a passive culture exists. This chapter offers strategies to address these key features.

Purpose	Strategies
Purpose and design	1 Plan the Questions
	2 Ask for Answers
	3 Mix It Up
	4 Serve and Return
	5 Probe the Thinking
	6 Make Them Meta
	7 Hinge Questions
	8 In Other Words
	9 Just Tell Them
Creating a positive culture	10 Wait Time
	11 Everybody Thinks
	12 Share the Love

Strategies for Purpose and Design

1. Plan the Questions

Having planned daily lessons for many years, I have been able to reflect upon and refine my planning process. Interestingly, I have found questioning to be at the heart of effective planning. After pinning down clear, explicit learning objectives for the lesson, I have found that using these two prompts were crucial to the process:

1   What questions should I ask the students, and with what purpose?

2   What questions might the students ask?

The first question makes me consider appropriate elaboration, retrieval and feedback questions. The second makes me think about which parts the students might find difficult so that I am better prepared to address them directly. These two questions often throw up the same answer, although considering both perspectives helps to ensure that I have explored all potential avenues.

These two prompts help to create a powerful framework for planning and help to us move away from a lesson plan that is a tick-list of tasks for students to do. As always, for this to become habitual, add the questions to your lesson planning pro forma or write them on a sticky note and stick it on your computer or desk as a reminder.

2. Ask for Answers

Not all questions are good questions. Take these for instance:

♦ Everybody got it?

♦ Everyone okay with this?

♦ Do we all understand?

♦ Are we all happy with this before we move on?

These types of questions are ineffective. They are an attempt to gain feedback and check for understanding but they fail for four reasons. Firstly, our knowledge of the Dunning–Kruger effect means that questions like these return false positives because the students think they are 'okay with this' when they aren't. Secondly, if a student is aware that they don't understand, they are unlikely to confess this in such a public forum. Thirdly, the answer to these questions is subjective – two students with similar levels of understanding may give different answers. Finally, these questions often tend to be asked in a rhetorical fashion, inherent in which is an inferred sense that the answer is yes.

When checking for understanding, a general rule of thumb is to avoid questions like these that have yes/no answers. Other supposedly more effective methods for checking understanding include self-assessment strategies such as thumbs up/down, 1–5 rating using the fingers and traffic lights (red, amber, green or RAG). While these methods do provide us with information, we need to be very careful when making judgements about student understanding which have arisen from self-assessment questions. That isn't to say there is no place for student self-assessment, just that we need to be mindful of the Dunning–Kruger effect and the subjective nature of the responses. These methods are actually assessing student confidence, not competence, but too often they are used as a measure of the latter.

Instead, pose your students a problem. For example, if they have been shown how to expand brackets, such as $2(x + 5)$, give them a minimally different problem to solve, such as $2(x + 6)$ (for more on this, revisit worked example pairs, in strategy 2, Chapter 2). This approach is preferable because it leaves no space for the Dunning–Kruger effect or subjective responses – the students can either solve the problem or not. The most effective way to do this is by using mini whiteboards so that all student responses can be checked. This is far more effective than asking, "Do you understand?"

3. Mix It Up

There have been many attempts to categorise the different types of questions and create frameworks for questioning, one of which is the distinction between open and closed questions. Closed questions have a single clear answer – for example, "Expand $2(x + 3)$." Open questions provoke thought and can be used as a starting point for further discussion – for example, "What is the same and what is different about $2(x + 3)$ and $2x + 3$?" Another way to categorise questions uses Bloom's taxonomy. This is often poorly depicted using the familiar pyramid, with lower order questions at the base through to the highest order at the top (Figure 4.2).

This brings us to one of the most pervasive misconceptions in teaching – that open or higher order questions are better than those that are closed or of a lower order, and that we should strive to ask only open or higher order questions in our classrooms. This is incorrect. All of these types of questions have value. It is as important to ask closed and lower order questions as it is to ask open and higher order questions because they serve different functions. Closed and lower order questions are particularly useful to check for understanding and retrieve knowledge, which is vital for learning (as we saw in Chapter 3); whereas open and higher order questions make students think, developing their reasoning skills and building conceptual understanding.

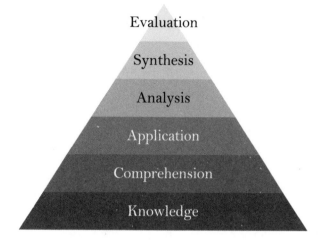

Figure 4.2. Bloom's taxonomy

The best approach is to mix it up by using all of these types of questions. Retrieval and feedback questions are more likely to be closed, while elaboration questions will be more open.

4. Serve and Return

During questioning, I often find myself instinctively defaulting to using the initiation-response-evaluation (IRE) model, whereby I initiate a question, a student responds and I make a final evaluative response before moving on. While this is appropriate at times, particularly when asking questions for retrieval and feedback, there is a need to develop opportunities for more extended dialogue.

This is referred to as 'dialogic questioning', where an initial question is followed up with a range of follow-up questions based on the student's response, designed to probe and deepen their thinking. When done well, it is like table tennis, with questions and answers being batted back and forth – or even better, when other students are involved, it is like a game of volleyball.

An example exchange could look like this:

T: What is a denominator?

S1: The bottom number of a fraction.

T: Yes. What does it tell us?

S1: The total number of parts.

T: Tell me more about these parts.

S2: All parts have to be the same size.

T: Can you repeat that using mathematical language?

S2: All parts must be of equal size.

T: Much better. Anything else to add?

S3: It's the number of parts of a whole.

T: Great. Why is this important? [Sketches the diagram below on the board] What is the denominator of the fraction represented here?

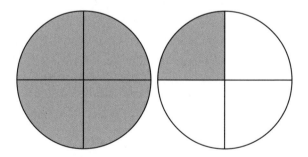

S3: Four because each of these circles is one whole.

T: Good. S4, can you link these ideas together in one sentence?

S4: The denominator is the number of equal parts of a whole.

T: Thank you. S1, please repeat.

S1 is now able to more coherently convey their understanding of what a denominator represents. Through relentless and focused questioning, the teacher is teasing out the key learning points. Facilitating whole-class dialogue is not easy. Given the vast amount of content to teach, it is tempting to move through content quickly due to lack of time. Extended dialogue is often a casualty. Yet research on the impact of dialogic teaching is positive: a primary project carried out by the Education Endowment Foundation found that it can add one month of progress to student learning in maths.[6] In the words of Doug Lemov, "the reward for a correct answer should always be a harder question".[7]

5. Probe the Thinking

If we truly want students to achieve deep understanding, we need to interrogate their thinking. We can do this by using probing questions. These are carefully crafted questions that students need to think hard about in order to formulate a response. They can help students to develop their reasoning skills and build conceptual understanding.

The beauty of probing questions is their flexibility. They can be used at many times and in many ways: with the whole class during explanation to orient attention and make the students think, while working with an individual student during practice, or as challenge and extension questions for those who are ready or to assess understanding. When used in this way – as exit tickets or as a test question, for example – they help us to identify whether a student has developed a conceptual understanding. If their understanding is shallow or superficial, they will struggle to form a response.

A further bonus is that they are easy to create using question stems (Table 4.1 lists some examples). One of my favourites is: "What is the same and what is different about …?" Consider these examples and ask yourself what the students will think about as a result of asking these questions:

What is the same and what is different about:

$$x^2 - 4x + 7 = 9 \text{ and } (x - 2)^2 + 3 = 9?$$

What is the same and what is different about:

$$y = x^2 - 4x + 7 \text{ and } x^2 - 4x + 7 = 9?$$

Table 4.1. Question stems to promote deeper thinking

Question stem	Example
… is the solution, what is the problem?	$5x$ is the solution, what is the problem?
… is the problem, what is the most common incorrect solution?	0.4×0.6 is the problem, what is the most common incorrect solution?
What is the same and what is different about … and …?	What is the same and what is different about 2130 g and 2.13 kg?
Combined with an incorrect worked example _____ solved this problem incorrectly. What advice would you give _____ so that he/she doesn't make this mistake again?	$4 \div \frac{1}{2} = 2$ Marine got this problem wrong. What advice would you give Marine so that she doesn't make this mistake again?
Change one thing about … so that …	Change one thing about $y = 2x + 5$ so that the line passes through the origin.
Show me an easy and a difficult example of …	Show me an easy and a difficult example of calculating the length of a side of a right-angled triangle using trigonometry.
Is it always, sometimes or never true that …	Is it always, sometimes or never true that a quadratic equation has two real roots.
Make up three problems to show you understand …	Make up three problems to show you understand how to find the nth term of a linear sequence.
Show me two ways of …	Show me two ways of solving $2(x + 3) = 14$.

Question stem	Example
Give me an example of … which has …	Give me an example of a shape which has the same perimeter and area.
Why do … all have the same solution?	Why do the derivatives of $x^2 + 3$, x^2 and $x^2 - 2$ all have the same solution?
How would you explain to an alien/a student who is absent/ your parents why …?	How would you explain to an alien why, when you divide by a fraction, you multiply by the reciprocal?

As a starting point, try to include at least one of these questions in each of your lessons.

6. Make Them Meta

Metacognition is yet another term in education that has many definitions. At its core it is 'thinking about thinking', although the Education Endowment Foundation define it as "the ability of students to independently plan, monitor, and evaluate their thinking and learning".[8] More generally, it can be considered as an awareness and understanding of our own thought processes. There is evidence to suggest that "fostering metacognition appears to be important to the development of mathematics competence",[9] and that it is particularly useful when solving problems.

The Education Endowment Foundation suggest that while demonstrating solving a problem, a teacher could model how to plan, monitor and evaluate their thinking by reflecting aloud using a series of prompts. These could include:

- ◆ What is this problem asking?
- ◆ Have I ever seen a mathematical problem like this before? What approaches to solving it did I try and were they successful?
- ◆ Could I represent the problem with a diagram or graph?

♦ Does my solution make sense when I re-read the problem?

♦ Do I need help or more information to solve this problem? Where could I find this?[10]

At the supermarket, you can buy toilet rolls in a pack of 4 or a pack of 9.

£2.49

£5.49

Which pack is better value?

Consider this problem which you want to solve with your students. Modelling your thinking in response to these prompts might look something like this:

T: This problem is asking me to work out whether four toilet rolls for £2.49 or nine for £5.49 is better value.

T: I have seen a problem like this before when I had to work out how many miles were travelled in one hour. Maybe I could find out how much it costs for one toilet roll in each pack.

T: In the miles problem, I knew that 141 miles were travelled in three hours. I worked out the distance travelled in one hour like this:

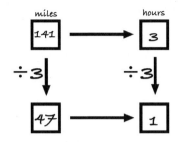

T: I can try doing this for my toilet roll problem:

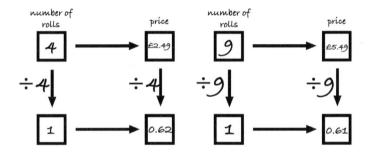

T: One toilet roll in the four-pack is 62p and in the nine-pack, 61p. I can check that my price per toilet roll is correct because 10 toilet rolls costing 60p would be £6, less one toilet roll is £5.40.

T: Have I solved the problem? No, because I need to decide which is the better value. I think that the nine-pack is better value because each toilet roll costs less.

The ultimate aim is that the students will internalise and automate these prompts. This starting point offers scaffolding to support them on this journey. To reduce the scaffold, provide the students with a copy of the prompts as they problem solve and ask them to record their responses. As they gain confidence, we can ask them to reflect aloud on their problem-solving approach using the prompts as a framework, with the hope that, eventually, the scaffold is no longer required.

7. Hinge Questions

A hinge question is a powerful way to design questions that serve our second purpose – gaining feedback on students' understanding. They allow us to judge whether the students are ready to practise after an explanation and whether they are ready to move on to more challenging work, having mastered what they are currently working on.

A good hinge question should:

♦ Be quick and easy for the teacher to ask.

♦ Be quick for the students to respond to – multiple choice questions are a popular option.

♦ Be designed so that a student is only likely to succeed if they understand.

♦ Be designed so that any incorrect responses inform the teacher about the misconceptions the students may have.

Consider the following example. You have been explaining how to subtract negative numbers. You want to check the students have understood this before they begin independent practice. You display the following hinge question with four possible options:

Calculate -6 – (-9)

A. -15

B. 3

C. 15

D. -3

If they have understood they would know that B is correct – the other responses are common misconceptions/incorrect answers. An important point here is that all the students should respond at the same time – they could use laminated ABCD cards,[11] mini whiteboards or vote by holding up the requisite number of fingers (1 for A, 2 for B, etc.). To help combat the temptation of students borrowing their neighbour's answer, count down from three, after allowing an appropriate length of thinking time, and expect everyone to reveal their answers simultaneously.

The most important part of a hinge question is what happens as a result of the feedback. If most students select the correct option, it is probably best to move on, making a mental note to pick up the few students who were incorrect through subsequent questioning or during practice. If there is a more even split between those who are correct and those who are not, things become a little more complicated. You could allow those who were correct to begin their practice, while recapping the teaching with those who were incorrect as a smaller group. Or you could discuss the four options, asking the students to elaborate on their thinking as part of a whole-class discussion. Discussing the options in alphabetical order, without divulging the correct solution, means that you can take a re-vote using a minimally different problem (e.g. -3 − (-8)) to see if the proportion of those answering correctly has improved. Deciding what to do next is the most important yet difficult part of using hinge questions.

Hinge questions are incredibly flexible. Not only can they be used as a check for understanding between the explanation and practice phases, but also to check prior knowledge at the start of a lesson and as exit tickets. The website https://diagnosticquestions.com has a bank of nearly 40,000 multiple choice questions that can be used in these ways.

8. In Other Words

In Chapter 2, we explored mathematical language and the complexities faced by students in accessing it. We can address this by using the phrase 'in other words' as a succinct and effective way of questioning students' understanding of maths vocabulary. When we use this phrase, it requires the students to respond by providing a definition of the key word being used. The exchanges below highlight what this might look like in action:

S: To find the area of a rectangle you multiply the length by the width.

T: Area. In other words?

S: The space inside a 2D shape.

T: One method that allows us to solve a quadratic equation is called completing the square. Quadratic. In other words?

S1: Something with a squared in.

T: What do you mean by something?

S1: An x^2.

T: Can anyone add to this?

S2: A term or expression where the highest power is 2.

T: S1, repeat.

You can either stop at this point and return to the focus of the lesson – which, in this case, is completing the square – or (depending on our assessment of the students' confidence) continue on this theme by asking them for examples on mini whiteboards. For instance, using concept/non-concept (see strategy 3 in Chapter 2) we could ask for examples of what a quadratic term, expression or equation is and what it isn't.

'In other words' is an excellent strategy for questioning and revisiting vocabulary and definitions. To be effective, it must be used consistently and frequently. Thus, while it can be used effectively in one classroom in isolation, it is at its most powerful as a whole-school strategy.[12]

9. Just Tell Them

Occasionally, I find myself unintentionally playing a game of 'guess what's in my mind' with the students. It starts with me asking a question that the students cannot answer. I respond by refining my question, asking additional questions that are more guided and less difficult until the students are able to answer. It slowly becomes a fairly pointless exchange. John Holt, author of *How Children Fail*, shares this experience of working with Ruth, a student who used this situation to her advantage:

I remember the day not long ago when Ruth opened my eyes. We had been doing math, and I was pleased with myself because, instead of telling her answers and showing her how to do problems, I was 'making her think' by asking her questions. It was slow work. Question after question met only silence. She said nothing, did nothing, just sat and looked at me through those glasses, and waited. Each time, I had to think of a question easier and more pointed than the last, until I finally found one so easy that she would feel safe in answering it. So we inched our way along until suddenly, looking at her as I waited for an answer to a question, I saw with a start that she was not at all puzzled by what I had asked her. In fact, she was not even thinking about it. She was coolly appraising me, weighing my patience, waiting for that next, sure-to-be-easier question.[13]

He realises that he's 'been had'. The student has learned how to get her teachers to do the work for her. When we find ourselves in this situation, the simplest way out is to just tell them the answer. The difficult part is realising that this is happening and stopping before we travel too far down this road. While telling the students the answer might not have been our desired outcome, we can follow this up by trying to work out why they couldn't answer the question – potential causes could be poor question design, lack of student knowledge or passivity.

Strategies for Creating a Positive Culture for Questioning

The strategies in the first part of this chapter provide a wealth of options for purposeful question design, yet they offer only half the story. Alongside them we need strategies that support the establishment of a positive culture for questioning – one that creates an environment where the students feel secure enough to contribute when asked a question and ensures that as many students as possible are engaged in the questioning process. Doug Lemov calls this the 'participation ratio', defined as a measure of who participates and how often: "Maximising it means getting all students involved in speaking, responding to questions, thinking actively, participating on cue, and processing ideas in writing, as often as possible."[14]

10. Wait Time

Wait time is the time between posing a question and taking a response from a student. It is the amount of time we give the students to think and form a response. Along with strategy 4 (Serve and Return), wait time suffers due to the conflict between content to cover and time available. This conflict causes the average wait time to be around one second.

Unfortunately, this often means that students give their first response, which is unlikely to be their best response. Indeed, for some students it is not enough time to formulate a response at all. Evidence suggests that increasing the wait time to a minimum of around three seconds allows sufficient time for better quality responses to be formed;[15] plus, it enables more students to participate. It is remarkably difficult to do because it rarely happens during a natural conversation – as a rule, we don't insist on people waiting three seconds before responding to the questions we ask. Creating a habit of silently counting to three in your head is a good way to ensure enough wait time is given.

Furthermore, research indicates that pauses of two or three seconds are also beneficial *after* the student has finished speaking (i.e. before we respond). It seems to give the student time to expand and reflect on their answer, or even in some cases, to backtrack, modify and further elaborate.[16]

11. Everybody Thinks

When I was at school, after the teacher had asked a question, the students would put their hands up to indicate that they had a contribution to make and the teacher would select from that pool of students. The problem with this is that, in general, it is the same group of students who raise their hands. Not only does this mean that a small group of students are doing most of the thinking, but also that the teacher's perception of the level of understanding of the class is being skewed by those who *can* answer.

Another issue is that when one student is giving a response, the other students may believe they are off the hook, leading to them disengaging. This strategy offers a refreshing look at a range of techniques available to avoid this happening, so that *everybody* thinks *all* of the time – regardless of whether all or one is called on to give a response.

The first technique is getting the whole class to respond to questions. This ensures that everyone thinks and avoids us gaining a distorted perception of what our students know. The most effective way to do this is using mini whiteboards. These are particularly useful for retrieval and feedback questions, but less so for elaboration questions as they tend to require lengthier, more unique responses.

Another option that particularly serves elaboration questions is to 'cold call' students. Ask a question, leave an appropriate amount of wait time and only then purposefully select a student to respond, irrespective of whether they have their hand up. This will ensure that all the students think because they never know whether a question will come their way. Some suggest adopting a 'no hands-up' policy alongside this strategy; however, my feeling is that there is useful information to be gained from seeing how many and whose hands are up, not least about the pitch of the question.

Rehearsal is another technique to ensure that everybody thinks and which works particularly well for elaboration questions. We can ask the students to rehearse their responses verbally in pairs or to write down their response before calling on one student to respond. While this takes more time, it has the added advantage of improving the quality of the responses.

The last technique is call and response, which prompts all students to respond in unison. It is more effective for closed retrieval questions. A cue should be agreed with the students so they know to all respond together. It might look something like this:

Teacher: *Call and response*, what are seven eights? 3, 2, 1 …

Class: 56.

The cue here is 'call and response' and a countdown to ensure unison. You can choose your own cue but ensure that it is clear and that the students are aware of it (Lemov suggests using the word 'class' as the cue). Nailing call and response will take practice, but it is still a useful tool for engaging all students.

12. Share the Love

Last, but not least, to truly build a positive culture for questioning and beyond, offer the students a way of showing their appreciation of contributions from their peers. In society, our default gesture for this is applause, but in the classroom this can be too disruptive. Commonly referred to as 'giving props', the best gestures are clear in their intent yet quiet enough that you can continue seamlessly. There are lots of ways to do this, including making up your own gesture as a class – repeatedly snapping your fingers tends to be most commonly used.

Reflective questions

♦ Which strategies will have the most powerful impact on your teaching?

♦ Are you planning by scripting questioning sequences that will give shape and direction to your lessons?

♦ Do you ensure that your questioning involves as many students as possible?

♦ Do you use the insight you gain from students' responses to challenge them further by asking follow-up questions?

♦ Do you spend time questioning when you could just tell them?

♦ Are you giving the students enough wait time so they have sufficient time to form a response and to encourage greater participation?

♦ Do you catch yourself asking rhetorical questions such as "Everyone got it?"

♦ Do you invite the students to contribute to classroom talk by sharing their strategies and mathematical thinking?

♦ Do you challenge the students to explore, argue and justify through your questioning?

♦ When you model solving a problem, do you also model your thought process as you go?

Endnotes

1   Barak Rosenshine, Principles of Instruction, p. 14.

2   See Edward Wragg and George Brown, *Questioning in the Secondary School* (Abingdon: Routledge, 2001).

3   Elizabeth Newton investigated 'tappers' and 'listeners' in The Rocky Road from Actions to Intentions, unpublished PhD dissertation, Stanford University, 1990.

4   *Source*: Ben Orlin, What Students See When They Look at Algebra, *Man with Bad Drawings* (22 June 2016). Available at: https://mathwithbaddrawings.com/2016/06/22/what-students-see-when-they-look-at-algebra/.

5   See Harold Pashler, Patrice M. Bain, Brian A. Bottge, Arthur Graesser, Kenneth Koedinger, Mark McDaniel and Janet Metcalfe, *Organizing Instruction and Study to Improve Student Learning: IES Practice Guide*. NCER 2007-2004 (Washington, DC: Institute of Education Sciences, 2007). Available at: https://ies.ed.gov/ncee/wwc/Docs/PracticeGuide/20072004.pdf, p. 23.

6   See https://educationendowmentfoundation.org.uk/projects-and-evaluation/projects/dialogic-teaching.

7   Quoted in Andy Tharby, Content, Thinking and Shaping: Three Principles for Working with Brighter Students, *Reflecting English* (30 January 2017). Available at: https://reflectingenglish.wordpress.com/2017/01/30/content-thinking-and-shaping-three-principles-for-working-with-brighter-students/.

8   Hodgen et al., *Improving Mathematics in Key Stages Two and Three: Guidance Report*, p. 20.

9   Henderson et al., *Improving Mathematics in Key Stages Two and Three: Evidence Review*, p. 17.

10 Henderson et al., *Improving Mathematics in Key Stages Two and Three: Evidence Review*, p. 21.

11 Plickers is a great digital formative assessment tool that does not require individual student devices: https://get.plickers.com.

12 Oasis Academy South Bank, a school in Central London, have nailed this, with teachers in all subjects using 'in other words' to great effect.

13 John Holt, *How Children Fail* (London: Pitman, 1964), p. 39. Cited in John Mason, Effective Questioning and Responding in the Mathematics Classroom (2010). Available at: https://www.researchgate.net/publication/234169730_Effective_Questioning_Responding.

14 Doug Lemov, *Teach Like a Champion 2.0*, pp. 234–235.

15 Andy Tharby, What Does Research Evidence Tell Us About Effective Questioning? *Research Schools Network* (24 May 2018). Available at: https://durrington.researchschool.org.uk/2018/05/24/what-does-research-evidence-tell-us-about-effective-questioning/.

16 Wiliam, *Embedded Formative Assessment*.

Chapter 5

Feedback

Feedback helps us to find out how we are doing, whether we are exploring a new city, perfecting our tennis serve or learning to play the guitar. Without this guidance we can struggle to make progress.

When trying to find your way to a famous monument in an unfamiliar city, what do you do? You might start by looking in a guidebook, checking a map or asking a local for directions. After setting off, you will keep your eyes peeled for landmarks along the way and compare these to the map. You might stop to ask someone if you are on the right track which may mean you need to change direction completely. Each of these interactions – with map, local and landmark – is a form of feedback.

As you repeat the route over and over – to and from your hotel – you will require less and less feedback until you can walk there without any guidance at all. Unless you plan to go further afield, of course. Then the cycle will start again. More feedback will be needed to guide you through the next stage of your journey – perhaps to a restaurant in the evening.[1]

The same principles apply to learning. First, we show our students what they are aiming for, before setting them on their journey, taking measures and adjusting their route via precise and timely feedback, so they arrive successfully at their destination. This may sound like a smooth journey with a few bumps along the way, but the reality is that it is more like captaining a ship at night in a storm.

The problem is that students do not learn exactly what we teach them. "No matter how well you describe something, how well you illustrate and explain it, students invent some new way to misunderstand what you have said," says Graham Nuthall in *The Hidden Lives of Learners*.[2] He goes on to say that 44–81% of all learning in a given lesson is unique – that is, it is learned by only a single student. Imagine trying to guide 30 ships from different ports to the same destination through a storm at night. Feedback helps to unpick the difference between what we think we have taught and what our students have learned.

There is plentiful research to highlight the importance and power of feedback. The Education Endowment Foundation Toolkit, which compares the efficacy of a range of educational interventions, scores feedback very highly – it has the potential to add eight months of progress to students' learning,[3] and these findings appear to apply to maths. Less good news is that the impact of feedback is variable. Worse news still is that it can have a negative effect – in some instances, feedback can result in poorer outcomes than if it wasn't given at all.[4] If we miss the mark with feedback, we risk damaging students' self-confidence – for example, giving grades to students allows them to compare themselves with each other. This can dent confidence, particularly for those whose grades were lower than expected. Rather than see this as a cue to work harder, they may give up entirely.

Feedback is wrapped up in many guises, each of which mean different things to different people. Formative feedback, formative assessment,[5] assessment for learning and responsive teaching are some of them. There is an argument that feedback and assessment are different – that feedback is the outcome of the process of assessment. I would agree, but the way in which we use these terms tends to conflate these differences.

In this chapter, we will consider effective feedback to be "information given to the learner and/or teacher about the learner's performance relative to learning goals",[6] which is "intended to modify his or her thinking or behaviour for the purpose of improving learning".[7] The term 'feedback' comes with baggage because it can be taken to mean marking. And marking can mean writing lengthy, repetitive comments or questions in students' books, often with an expectation that the students should respond, to which you respond, to which they respond ... Shaun Allison and Andy Tharby liken this to sending letters via the Royal Mail when you could pick up the phone: "very civilized but hideously slow and inefficient".[8]

There are many approaches to feedback that do not require writing comments in students' books which we will explore in this chapter. Recently, there has been a drive to reduce this practice. In 2016, the Independent Teacher Workload Review Group reported that:

Marking has evolved into an unhelpful burden for teachers, when the time it takes is not repaid in positive impact on pupils' progress. This is frequently because it is serving a different purpose such as demonstrating teacher performance or to satisfy the requirements of other, mainly adult, audiences. Too often, it is the marking itself which is being monitored and commented on by leaders rather than pupil outcomes and progress as a result of quality feedback."[9]

In 2018, the Department for Education published an exemplar feedback policy which spelled out that "a teacher should only write in a pupil's book if it is going to impact on progress".[10]

With specific application to maths, the National Centre for Excellence in the Teaching of Mathematics state:

♦ It should not be a routine expectation that next steps or targets be written into students' books. The next lesson should be designed to take account of the next steps

♦ It should not be an expectation that recurring errors or common misconceptions be addressed through individual comments in individual student's books. Where a number of students share a misconception, this should be addressed in lesson time.[11]

Henri Picciotto, an American educator, hits the nail on the head when he says, "When grading, you are working for one student. When planning, you are working for the whole class. Keep that in mind when you are budgeting your time."[12] So, let's mark less – it's high effort for low impact. Instead, let's utilise other approaches to feedback that flip this round so we put in less effort for greater impact.

Feedback comes in many shapes and sizes. It can be verbal, written or simply arise from a student marking their own work. It can come from the teacher or from peers. It can be an explanation, additional practice, an example or another lesson. It doesn't need to be a comment and it doesn't need to be personalised for every student.[13] Most importantly, when operating effectively, feedback is a cyclical process between teacher and student(s) whereby the ultimate aim is that the teacher adapts their teaching as a result of the feedback, which results in a change to student thinking.

Essentially, we are trying to identify gaps or misconceptions in understanding. We respond to this information by adjusting our teaching, so that we close the gap or unpick the misconception. Let's consider a practical example. You are teaching students how to find the area of a triangle. Having finished your explanation you carry out a whole-class check for understanding using mini whiteboards to see if the students are ready to begin independent practice. This reveals that the students hold a misconception that it is possible to calculate the area of a triangle using the lengths of two sides rather than the base and perpendicular height. Instead of allowing them to begin to practise, you adapt by explicitly reteaching this aspect so the students change their thinking.

There is an important and interesting side effect of us being responsive. Harry Fletcher-Wood suggests that "people who believe they are interacting with someone responsive tend to feel better and do better".[14] Therefore, if we ensure that we close the feedback cycle by adapting our teaching, our students may feel, and become, more successful.

Feedback can occur over varying time frames. A check for understanding in the lesson using mini whiteboards provides feedback in a matter of seconds, whereas using information gained from formal testing to drive curriculum change may take place over years. Dylan Wiliam, the godfather of formative assessment, tells us that it is most effective when closer to learning. The shorter the cycle, the bigger the impact. The most effective time frame is within and between lessons.[15]

There is another major problem with feedback of which we must be wary. When we gather information about learning during or directly after the learning has taken place, we are not actually measuring *learning* – we are measuring *performance*. Given that learning is a permanent change in long-term memory, if we want to measure learning, we must do this after some time has passed. At the end of a lesson on finding the mean from a frequency table, it is likely that the students will be able to demonstrate that they can find the mean from a frequency table. But can they still demonstrate this one week, one month or even six months later?

The measurement of performance is still of some use to us: if the students show they do not have the knowledge when we measure their performance, we can safely infer that they have not learned anything because they will not be able to recall this at a later stage. However, when the students do perform well in the moment we must regard this with caution: it does not mean learning has taken place unless they can replicate it at a later stage. Setting topic homeworks and tests with a delay of several weeks or months can help us to draw inferences about learning. As the celebrated maths educator John Mason says, "teaching takes place in time, learning takes place over time".[16]

With great power comes great responsibility. Feedback has great power. Wiliam once calculated: "If you price teachers' time appropriately, in England we spend about two and a half billion pounds a year on feedback and it has almost no effect on student achievement."[17] If we can uncouple feedback from onerous marking policies and take account of the fact that to measure learning we need to delay our assessment, then we can avoid it becoming ineffective.

Before we move on to strategies that help us to harness the power of feedback, here are some overarching principles from Wiliam:

♦ Feedback should cause thinking by the student.[18]

♦ The major purpose of feedback should be to improve the student, not the work.[19]

♦ Feedback should be more work for the student than for the teacher.[20]

Wiliam and Christodoulou provide an example whereby, instead of marking work with ticks and crosses, they suggest telling the student: "Five of these are wrong. You find them; you fix them."[21] This feedback causes the student to think, encourages them to identify errors themselves and is more work for them than for us.

When feedback fails it is often because it doesn't fulfil these principles. The feedback results in a lack of action by the students because it doesn't make them think. Perhaps they don't even understand it. Michael Pershan, an American maths educator, calls this "better luck next time" feedback.[22] It basically says: you got this wrong, it should have been this, don't do it again.

Well done, Amandeep, you got most of these correct. You should have multiplied in question 5 rather than added. Better luck next time!

This is unhelpful feedback. Unless it's a computation mistake, students don't do this on purpose; if Amandeep had known how to do it, she wouldn't have made the mistake. Pointing this out is not moving her forward.

Strategies

Feedback can occur immediately within the lesson or during the next lesson once we've had an opportunity to look at the work the students have completed. The strategies in this chapter are grouped in this way: those designed for minute-by-minute feedback to inform responsiveness *during* the lesson, and day-by-day strategies to inform planning *between* lessons.

Firstly, we will consider what it means to plan for feedback.

Planning for Feedback

A good foundation when planning for feedback is to aim to prove that students *don't* understand. In this way, we will probe harder to identify gaps and misconceptions. And if we fail to find them, we will know that they understand. It is useful to ask the following questions when planning:

♦ Does the plan respond to previous feedback? (For example, exit tickets from the last lesson identified that the students can factorise correctly when the common factor is a number or a letter, but when the common factor is composed of both they often only identify the number. Consequently, this is explicitly retaught during the lesson followed by lots of practice.)

♦ When will there be opportunities for feedback during the lesson?

♦ What type/time frame/form will this take?

♦ Has time been allocated for the students to respond to written feedback if necessary?

The Feedback Mindset

We must take into consideration the impact that feedback can have on students' confidence. If it is poorly timed or pitched, feedback can be ignored or, worse still, cause students to reduce their effort. Creating a culture whereby students understand the purpose of feedback is important. Reminding them of this on a regular basis using the statements below can help:

I am giving you this feedback because I believe in you.

I am giving you this feedback because I know you can get better at this.

I am giving you this feedback because I know you can succeed.

I am giving you this feedback because I believe you can do this.

We can do this in different ways at different points in the lesson. Here are some examples:

◆ *Verbally* – to an individual student when sharing their work with the whole group using a visualiser: "We are going to give Jamal some feedback so that he can nail solving equations."

◆ *Verbally* – to the whole class before giving them individual feedback.

◆ *Written* – in their book or on a sticky note for a student who needs it.

A research analysis reveals that considerable enhancements in student achievement are possible when teachers use minute-by-minute and day-by-day formative assessment practices.[23] Consequently, our strategies focus on these timeframes.

Purpose	Strategies
Minute-by-minute feedback strategies to inform responses *during* the lesson	1 Writing on Whiteboards 2 Immediate Feedback 3 Live Feedback 4 Verbal Feedback 5 Check for Reasonableness 6 View with a Visualiser 7 Responsive Round-up
Day-by-day feedback strategies to inform planning *between* lessons	8 Exit Tickets 9 Whole-Class Feedback 10 Raise the Responsibility 11 Codes for Common Issues

Minute-by-minute feedback strategies to inform responses *during* the lesson

1. Writing on Whiteboards

The most effective way to gain real-time feedback from all students during the lesson is by using mini whiteboards. In my humble opinion, they are the single most powerful implement we have to hand. Tom Sherrington agrees, highlighting them as being the number one bit of classroom kit.[24] They are effective because they make all the students think, provide us with feedback from all the students and seem to make the students more comfortable with taking risks and making mistakes (probably due to the easy edit and wipe-clean aspect).

There are two factors that make or break the power of mini whiteboards: how we respond and how we build effective routines for their use. Let's imagine that mini whiteboards are being used alongside the worked example pairs from strategy 2 in Chapter 2. When the students show their boards, there are many possible outcomes and each one requires a different response:

1   If the majority of the class are correct, it is best to move on. Make a mental note of who did not give the correct response so that you can check their responses to the next question or check in with them at the start of independent practice.

2   If more than a handful of students are displaying an incorrect solution, it is time to pause and adapt accordingly. This could mean asking students to explain their responses. I often take a couple of mini whiteboards with different responses from students and hold them up at the front of the class. I ask the students to explain which one they think is correct and why.

3   When very few students provide a correct response, this is a strong signal that we need to reteach the topic.

For each of these outcomes, flexibility is key. Remember that the worst outcome is for there to be no response.

It is important to establish good routines for the use of mini whiteboards. Much like any routine in the classroom, the more often they are used, the more successful they become. Use mini whiteboards regularly so this process is automated. My routine goes something like this:

1 Display the problem on the board. There is no need to read it out if it is displayed clearly.

2 Tell the students they have 10 seconds to write their response (or longer, depending on the complexity of the problem).

3 Start the countdown loudly: "10, 9, 8 ..." to encourage quick engagement, then continue counting silently so as not to distract the students from their work.

4 Increase the volume towards the end of the time: "3, 2, 1 ..." and then say, "Show me, show me, show me."

The expectation is that all the students will hold up their board at the same time. If a student displays their board before I say "show me", I ask them to lower it to reduce the potential for copying. It is important that all the students offer a response – encourage them to give their best effort. I tend to avoid using the terms 'guess', 'guestimate' and 'mathematical guess' because they refer to guessing; I want my students to think hard, not guess.

If you are using mini whiteboards for the first time, you may find that the students decide to draw or write something other than an appropriate response on their board. Be ready for this – plan how you will respond. You can use your school behaviour policy as you would in any other circumstance to sanction this.

There is a limit to the usefulness of mini whiteboards due to their size. If you want the students to solve a multi-step problem or offer a longer response there is an equally effective tool – large whiteboards. When I joined my last school, the first thing I requested was to have several large whiteboards mounted on each of my classroom walls.

There are many benefits to using large whiteboards, the most relevant being instant feedback – we can immediately see what every student is doing at each step of their working. They boost collaboration by enabling pairs or threes to work at each board. We can use the students' working to unpick misconceptions or highlight errors. Another option is to leave their calculations on the whiteboards until the next lesson and, as a starter, remove a line of their working and ask them to complete it or to identify which solutions are correct and why. In my experience, the students can be more engaged at whiteboards than when they are working at their desks, and seem more comfortable to make mistakes. Again, this is likely to be linked to the lack of permanency of their work.

They are particularly useful for exam questions and when teaching A level, where most problems require lots of working out. The only drawback is cost: large whiteboards are not cheap, whereas you can get a class set of mini whiteboards and pens for around £30. A less effective but cheaper alternative is to use magic whiteboards – large plastic sheets that stick to any surface that you can write on, rub off and reuse.

2. Immediate Feedback

You are about to take off from London Heathrow on a flight to New York City. Inexplicably, your pilot taxies to the wrong runway and, in a matter of minutes, you are flying towards mainland Europe. The further you fly in the wrong direction, the harder it is for the pilot to undo his mistake.

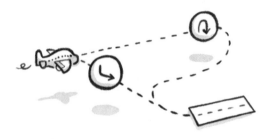

This exemplifies why the provision of feedback *during* practice is so important. The further our students go off track, the further they compound the errors and misconceptions they make. On the flip side, a huge mistake can also provide a valuable salutary lesson – we can hope that, in the future, our pilot will pay closer attention to air traffic control's instructions.

The hard part is to strike a balance between giving and withholding feedback so the students have enough room to think for themselves but enough guidance to avoid embedding misconceptions. David Didau likens an over-reliance on feedback to using a satnav over a physical map. If you make a mistake when using a satnav you get immediate feedback in the form of an automatic adjustment to your route, but you fail to learn anything about the road layout that could help if you were stuck without your satnav. Using a map takes more effort, but the more you use a map, the more you begin to memorise routes.[25] One way to approach this problem is to offer feedback more readily at the start of a learning episode, with a view to withdrawing it as you move forward. If our feedback is effective, the students should need it less as their knowledge and understanding starts to improve.

Immediate feedback is a feature of deliberate practice which we discussed in Chapter 3. In the context of deliberate practice, feedback is normally given by the expert during a one-to-one taught session. While we can't always offer this level of individual feedback, we can routinely help students to self or peer check by providing them with the solutions while they practise. Waiting until the end of the lesson is too late, for the reasons explained here.

When students are self-checking, solutions to problems can be given on the back of worksheets, on a separate sheet or on the main board, and if using textbooks they can LUBB (Look it Up in the Back of the Book). Peer checking takes a little more effort to facilitate but it can be more effective. This can be done by creating two different sets of problems, one for each member of a pair; one set of problems have the solutions to the second set, and vice versa. The students can then work in pairs to give immediate feedback. Either way, if they come up with an incorrect solution, it is important for them to try to work out why.

Providing solutions alongside a task, rather than at the end, isn't a natural thing for us to do. We may feel that it is being too helpful, or that it removes the challenge or encourages copying. This can be overcome by having high expectations of showing working out and a classroom culture whereby the students understand that they are only cheating themselves if they copy solutions without attempting the problems.

3. Live Feedback

While students are practising, patrol the room to inspect their progress, checking in first with those who were identified as needing support during the check for understanding. Giving feedback could be as simple as using a pen to tick and cross; however, a more effective approach is to arm yourself with highlighter pens:

♦ Use green to highlight any piece of work that is particularly impressive. It could be that a student has demonstrated exemplary workings, an impressive explanation or they have responded well to previous feedback.

♦ Use yellow to indicate that the solution is correct but that something else can be improved. This could be that they have written something along the lines of $3 + 4 = 7 \times 5 = 35$ in their workings or they have failed to check their solution for reasonableness (see strategy 5).

♦ Use orange to indicate that their solution is incorrect – the student must then correct it. Providing the correct solution can help them to locate their error(s).

When using yellow or orange, revisit the student after five minutes or so to see how they have got on. Using highlighters is a great way to speed up live feedback, but remember to provide the class with a colour-coded key that explains what each colour means.

Codes for Common Issues (strategy 11) provides yet another structure to make live feedback super effective.

4. Verbal Feedback

Verbal feedback is the bread and butter of the maths teacher – it should never be underestimated and nor should it require a verbal feedback stamp in the students' books. Stamps are for accountability, not student performance. Even Ofsted has sought to verify their position on this matter stating that "Ofsted do not expect to see any written record of oral feedback".[26] Verbal feedback should be just that – the teacher telling the student how to get better.

When giving verbal feedback, there is a real risk that the moment you move away, the student will forget everything you have said and your words of feedback wisdom become lost in the ether. Do not fear – there is an easy way to avoid this. After discussing the work, ask the student to repeat the feedback back to you in their own words. Once you are sure they understand, ask them to tell you the first thing they are going to do. Let them get started and, if possible, return after a few minutes to check they are on course.

By verbalising the feedback and then committing to action, there is a far greater chance that the student will respond successfully. When giving feedback like this, or in fact in any other way, it is important to keep it concise. If it is unfocused, the student may struggle to assimilate or act upon it.

5. Check for Reasonableness

When the new maths GCSE was introduced I became an examiner to familiarise myself with how the exam board was assessing the new curriculum. Having marked my allocated batch of papers, I reflected on what I had learned from the experience. One thing struck me above anything else: students are terrible at judging the validity of their solutions! Time and time again, candidates provided solutions that were blatantly wrong, and which in most cases would have been easily identified as being incorrect if they had done a quick validity check.

Consider the examples in Figure 5.1.

Calculate the missing length.

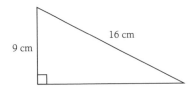

16 cm

9 cm

Give your answer to 3 significant figures.

$$16^2 + 9^2 = 337$$
$$\sqrt{337} = 18.357\ldots$$

Answer _____ 18.4 _____ cm

---

140 runners are given a bottle of water at the finish line. How many packs of 6 bottles will the organisers need to buy so that every runner gets a bottle?

$$140 \div 6 = 23.33\ldots$$

Answer __23__

The table shows the amount of pocket money a group of children is given per week. Work out an estimate for the mean amount of weekly pocket money received.

Pocket money (P) in £	Frequency		
0 < P ≤ 5	11	2.5	27.5
5 < P ≤ 10	22	7.5	165
10 < P ≤ 15	8	12.5	100
15 < P ≤ 20	2	17.5	35
		4	327.5

$$327.5 \div 4 = \underline{81.875}$$

Complete the table of values given $y = 3x - 1$

x	-3	-2	-1	0	1	2	3
y	-10	-7	2	-1	2	5	8

Figure 5.1. Examples of scenarios in which a check for reasonableness would have exposed an incorrect solution

For the triangle problem, the calculated length of side y is longer than the hypotenuse. Next, the estimated mean is well outside the range of the data. Multiplication would have shown that 23 packs wouldn't provide enough bottles of water and, glancing at the completed table of values, the value for y when $x = -1$ sticks out because it doesn't follow the pattern.

Let's be clear here: we're talking about more than a casual check. To most students, checking their solutions is interpreted as meaning, at best, covering their workings and solving the problem again or, at worst, reading through their workings. In both cases they are highly likely to replicate the original errors. What we want them to do is hard. We want them to check the validity of their solution in the context of the problem – to check the magnitude of their solution, to use inverse operations and substitution, to check for anomalies in patterns. This is powerful feedback for students because it circumvents their reliance on us.

It is useful to use a phrase with the students to signal this. My default was 'check for reasonableness' but it is quite cumbersome. 'Sensible solution'[27] or 'check for coherence' are better options. Whichever phrase you use, the key is to clearly explain what it means and use it regularly. After modelling a worked example I would ask, "How could we do a check for reasonableness?" Before helping students during independent practice I would ask, "Have you done a check for reasonableness?" When marking work I would highlight scenarios where the students had produced an incorrect solution that could have been identified using a check for reasonableness by writing 'CfR' (see strategy 11).

6. View with a Visualiser

In strategy 1, I shared my number one resource in the classroom – mini whiteboards. My second is a visualiser, for which you need a PC and projector. Visualisers are becoming increasingly common in classrooms. As well as being a useful tool for modelling, they provide timely and effective feedback by enabling student work to be projected in the moment. This can be work of a student in the class or from another class. Guided by the teacher, the students can discuss the effectiveness of the work displayed and give suggestions for improvements. While the feedback is generally directed towards the one pupil whose work is displayed, if the rest of the class is tasked with comparing their own work to the projected work, the benefits ripple throughout the class.

7. Responsive Round-up

It is common practice for us to share solutions with students at the end of the lesson. Whether we use this approach or share solutions during practice (as in strategy 2), what is most important is that we are responsive – we try to get a sense of any problems that caused our students difficulties.

Do this by asking the students to write on a mini whiteboard the number of the problem they would like to go through as a class. If numerous students give the same number, it is worth working on that question with the whole class. This is less helpful if they give different numbers.

In addition, it is useful to gain a measure of success. Decide on a benchmark (e.g. 7 out of 10) and ask the students to raise their hand if they got 7 or more correct. This can inform your next steps.

Day-by-Day Feedback Strategies to Inform Planning *Between* Lessons

8. Exit Tickets

Exit tickets are one of the top strategies for feedback. Their purpose is to inform future planning by checking understanding at the end of a lesson. To create their content, we can refer to our carefully chosen learning objective(s) and identify a couple of problems that we want the students to be able to solve. The students solve these problems on a piece of paper and hand them in on their way out of the lesson. After the lesson, it can take anything from five to fifteen minutes to assess them, depending on the volume and complexity of the questions.

We don't need to mark exit tickets in the traditional sense. Examine each ticket and place them into piles – for example, two piles (correct and incorrect) or three piles (incorrect, some correct, all correct). The size of the piles can then inform your next steps, which will vary from speaking to an individual student, creating a relevant starter to highlight an issue or reteaching the lesson. What you then do with the tickets is up to you: ask the students to correct them if there are lots of errors, use a visualiser to display a few or bin them. Mine would pretty much always end up in the bin.

Be flexible. Lessons don't always go to plan and you may want to change the problems you had planned to use. Sometimes, particularly when introducing a new topic, I am unsure how far my students will progress in a lesson so I might not explicitly plan the problem I want them to solve. Either way, I always have a stash of A5 scrap paper to hand ready to be used for exit tickets. I write the problems on the board and the students can complete them on the scrap paper – don't let them forget to add their name.

Some tips for supercharging the impact of exit tickets include:

♦ Share the rationale with students – that they help us to understand what they know from the lesson and what we might need to teach next, rather than being an assessment tool that we use to judge their ability.

♦ Collect and check exit tickets at the door as the students are on the way out of the classroom. It is an exit ticket in the literal sense – they cannot leave the room without it. This highlights to them the importance of the task and enables us to ensure that all students complete the ticket properly. If they haven't completed it well enough, make them stay behind to do it or come back during breaktime. This will ensure that they make a better job of it next time.

♦ The internet is full of ideas for exit tickets. Too full. I tend to make them myself. That said, the AlgebraByExample materials are a great source for exit tickets and can be used as a template for strands beyond algebra.[28]

9. Whole-Class Feedback

When marking, instead of writing individual comments on each piece of work, record feedback for the whole class. It is much quicker to do while still maintaining the required impact. There are two parts to this process: firstly, make notes about the work and, secondly, respond to the information gleaned by adapting the next lesson.

The notes could include some or all of the following:

♦ Misconceptions and gaps in knowledge with actions:

◊ What are the misconceptions and/or gaps in knowledge?

◊ Who has them? All/some/individuals?

◊ What actions will you take as a result of this feedback? (See below for some suggestions.)

♦ Work to share: excellent presentation, an interesting strategy, a misconception, etc.

♦ Rewards:

◊ For whom?

◊ Why do they deserve a reward? (This could be related to attainment, effort or presentation.)

◊ What will the reward be?

♦ Concerns:

◊ About whom?

◊ Why are you concerned? (This could be related to attainment, effort or presentation.)

◊ How will you address this?

Once you get a sense of what information is most important, you can create a template to record this more efficiently (Figure 5.2).[29]

Class: 9x3 Date: 19th October	Feedback on: Weekly quiz
Misconceptions and gaps in knowledge with actions: Most got number 7 wrong. Create an incorrect worked example with worked example pair and student self-explanation as a starter for next lesson. Remember to ask students to give advice so they don't make the same mistake again. Trish has a misconception about $2x^2$ and $(2x)^2$. Find time to talk with her and share similar example anonymously with group.	**Rewards (who, why and what):** Trish: amazing effort – postcard home Dipak: fab explanation – public praise, share with class via visualiser and double merit points Fatima and Bob: all correct – merit points
Work to share: Dipak's explanation Trish's classic misconception	**Concerns (who, why and what):** Jordan: not complete – detention Iram: poor effort – talk to her and phone home Phil: lazy presentation – detention Remind all to show working out!

Figure 5.2. Recording whole-class feedback

The second part is to be responsive – use this information to adapt your next lesson. You will likely find that there are pieces of feedback that apply to numerous students. There are several ways to share this with the class in the next lesson. Here are a few ideas that ensure the students are thinking about the feedback:

♦ Create a set of problems that explicitly address the issues found that all the students complete, perhaps as a starter.

♦ Collect together all of the unique incorrect solutions and create a set of incorrect worked examples for the students to correct. Remember to get them to answer the killer question: what advice would they give the student so they don't make the same mistake again?

♦ Give them a list of feedback comments and get them to work out which applies to them.

♦ Reteach something if necessary – if several students demonstrated the same errors or misconceptions.

♦ Use a visualiser to share and improve specific pieces of work, followed up with a minimally different question for the students to complete.

♦ Write a number on each piece of work to represent the number of errors made. Follow up by asking the students to find and fix them.

10. Raise the Responsibility

The long-term goal is for students to take greater responsibility in the feedback cycle. We need to help them by offering structures that allow them to make their own decisions about getting feedback.

One way to do this is to have a box in your room for the students to opt to put their book into if they wish to get feedback about a specific question. They circle the problem with a yellow whiteboard pen and write why they would like feedback before placing their open book in the box. I would then check their work before the next lesson. It is useful to keep a record of who has and hasn't used the box.

Another idea is to get students to share feedback about their homework by listing the problems they found difficult on the main board at the start of the lesson.[30]

11. Codes for Common Issues

Students are prone to repetitively making the same errors. This can lead to us writing the same feedback over and over again in different books:

Redo this diagram with a ruler and pencil.

Please add units.

Please complete this solution.

This led to me creating a code system so that I could continue to convey high expectations for student work, while reducing the time it took to do so. Crucially, each code results in a corresponding student action to ensure that they are made to think. Ensure you allocate some time for the students to act on the feedback – if your school has dedicated improvement and reflection time (DIRT), this is a perfect time in which to do it.

Table 5.1. Examples of codes for common issues

Code	Meaning	Student action
★	Excellent work	This piece of work is fabulous. Work out why and write it down.
SW	Show working	Redo this question showing your working.
CfR	Check for reasonableness[31]	Your solution is clearly incorrect. Work out why by doing a check for reasonableness and explain your thinking in words.
ft	Follow through	You have used the correct method but you have made an incorrect calculation. Find it and fix it.
+	Needs more	This problem is not yet finished – there is more to do. Finish it. How can you avoid doing this in the future?

Code	Meaning	Student action
?	Unclear	It is unclear what the initial problem was and/or how you solved it and/or what your solution is. Redo it, ensuring you write down the initial problem, explain each step and underline your solution.
u	Units are missing	Add the correct units to your solution.
r	Rounding	Round your solution to an appropriate degree of accuracy. Don't forget to include the degree of accuracy. For example = 4.06 (to 3 sig figs).
=	Not equal	You have incorrectly used the equals sign. For example, $4 + 3 = 7 \times 2 = 14$. $4 + 3 \neq 14$. Find it and fix it.
RtQ	Read the question	You have solved a different problem to the one given. Redo it. How can you avoid doing this in the future?
RP	Use a ruler and/or pencil	Redo this diagram using a ruler and/or pencil.

Either use these examples as a starting point or create your own. Remember to print a copy for the students to refer to. You can also use these codes when live marking or when inspecting work to inform whole-class feedback.

You will see that the code for 'follow through' as used in exam mark schemes is included. You can supercharge this strategy by regularly using exam mark scheme abbreviations and adding them to your regular codes. In this way, the students become familiar with their meaning and use so that, in time, they can use an exam mark scheme to assess their own exam and test papers. As Dylan Wiliam says, "the best person to mark a test is the person who just took it".[32]

These strategies attempt to harness the powerful impact of feedback, while avoiding the pitfalls. However, what really matters with feedback is the relationship between us and our students. The same feedback given to two students can make one try harder and cause the other to give up – it is our job to know which is which.[33]

Finally, we must remember that in all these instances the feedback we get is about performance not learning, unless the task is delayed. I would suggest a delay of at least a month – the real test is if they still know it six months down the line!

Reflective questions

♦ Which strategies will have the most powerful impact on your teaching?

♦ How can you make sure that the students understand the feedback you give them?

♦ How can you ensure that the feedback makes the students think and move forward with their thinking?

♦ How do you shape feedback so that the students engage and respond with action?

♦ Is your feedback more work for the student than for you?

♦ How can you attempt to change the student and not the work?

♦ Have you considered what form of feedback is most effective at different times?

♦ How can you check that your students are not over-reliant on feedback?

♦ How does feedback inform your planning (e.g. exit tickets, whole-class feedback)?

♦ If you use peer or self-feedback, how do you ensure that it doesn't compound misconceptions?

Endnotes

1   Allison and Tharby, *Making Every Lesson Count*, pp. 166–167.

2   Nuthall, *The Hidden Lives of Learners*, p. 24.

3   See https://educationendowmentfoundation.org.uk/toolkit/toolkit-a-z/feedback/.

4   Avraham N. Kluger and Angelo S. DeNisi, The Effects of Feedback Interventions on Performance: A Historical Review, a Meta-Analysis, and a Preliminary Feedback Intervention Theory, *Psychological Bulletin* 119(2) (1996): 254–284. Available at: https://www.researchgate. net/publication/232458848_The_Effects_of_Feedback_Interventions_on_Performance_ A_Historical_Review_a_Meta-Analysis_and_a_Preliminary_Feedback_Intervention_Theory.

5   Formative assessment can also refer to a broader process where feedback is a primary component.

6   Education Endowment Foundation, Feedback: Teaching & Learning Toolkit (28 September 2018). Available at: https://educationendowmentfoundation.org.uk/pdf/generate/?u=https:// educationendowmentfoundation.org.uk/pdf/toolkit/?id=131&t=Teaching%20and%20 Learning%20Toolkit&e=131&s=, p. 2.

7   Valerie J. Shute, Focus on Formative Feedback, *Review of Educational Research* 78(1) (2008): 153–189. Available at: https://www.researchgate.net/publication/220017728_Focus_on_ Formative_Feedback, p. 154.

8   Allison and Tharby, *Making Every Lesson Count*, p. 182.

9   Department for Education, *Eliminating Unnecessary Workload Around Marking: Report of the Independent Teacher Workload Review Group* (March 2016). Available at: https://www.gov.uk/ government/publications/reducing-teacher-workload-marking-policy-review-group-report, p. 6.

10 See Department for Education, Practical Tools: Example of a Feedback Policy (Secondary School) (July 2018). Available at: https://www.gov.uk/government/publications/ feedback-and-marking-reducing-teacher-workload, p. 2.

11 See National Centre for Excellence in the Teaching of Mathematics, Guidance on Marking and Feedback for Secondary Mathematics Teaching (October 2016). Available at: https://www. ncetm.org.uk/public/files/40764571/Secondary+Marking+Guidance+(October+2016).pdf, p. 1.

12 See Henri Picciotto, More Catchphrases, *Henri's Math Education Blog* (8 November 2018). Available at: https://blog.mathed.page/2018/11/08/more-catchphrases/.

13 Michael Pershan writes well about this in Feedbackless Feedback, *Teaching with Problems* (26 May 2017). Available at: https://problemproblems.wordpress.com/2017/05/26/ feedbackless-feedback/.

14 Harry Fletcher-Wood, What is Responsive Teaching?, *Improving Teaching* (3 June 2018). Available at: https://improvingteaching.co.uk/2018/06/03/what-is-responsive-teaching/.

15 Dylan Wiliam, Assessment for Learning: Why, What and How? Edited transcript of a talk given at the Cambridge Assessment Network Conference at the Faculty of Education, University of Cambridge, 15 September 2006. Available at: http://www.dylanwiliam.org/ Dylan_Wiliams_website/Papers.html, p. 7.

16 Quoted in Peter Griffin, Teaching Takes Place in Time, Learning Takes Place Over Time, *Mathematics Teaching* 126 (1989): 12–13.

17 Dylan Wiliam and Daisy Christodoulou, Assessment, Marking and Feedback. In Carl Hendrick and Robin Macpherson (eds), *What Does This Look Like in the Classroom?* (Woodbridge: John Catt Educational, 2017), pp. 22–44 at p. 27.

18 Wiliam, *Embedded Formative Assessment*, p. 132.

19 Wiliam and Christodoulou, Assessment, Marking and Feedback, p. 29.

20 Wiliam, *Embedded Formative Assessment*, p. 132.

21 Wiliam and Christodoulou, Assessment, Marking and Feedback, p. 29.

22 Michael Pershan: Beyond 'Better-Luck-Next-Time' Feedback, *Heinemann Blog* (12 May 2016). Available at: https://blog.heinemann.com/mpershan-feedbackupdate-5-12.

23 See Wiliam, Content *Then* Process; and National Council of Teachers of Mathematics, Five 'Key Strategies' for Effective Formative Assessment. Research Brief (2007). Available at: https://www.nctm.org/uploadedFiles/Research_and_Advocacy/research_brief_and_clips/Research_brief_04_-_Five_Key%20Strategies.pdf.

24 See Tom Sherrington, The Number 1 Bit of Classroom Kit: Mini-Whiteboards, *teacherhead* (28 August 2012). Available at: https://teacherhead.com/2012/08/28/the-number-1-bit-of-classroom-kit-mini-whiteboards/).

25 See David Didau, The Feedback Continuum: Why Reducing Feedback Helps Students Learn, *The Learning Spy* (1 November 2016). Available at: https://learningspy.co.uk/learning/the-feedback-continuum/.

26 Department for Education, *Eliminating Unnecessary Workload Around Marking*, p. 9.

27 Thanks to Ben Gordon for this suggestion.

28 See https://math.serpmedia.org/algebra_by_example/download_center.html.

29 Hat tip to Greg Thornton, Rob Stewart and Ben Gordon for sharing their templates.

30 Magpied from Greg Ashman who writes an excellent blog: https://gregashman.wordpress.com.

31 See strategy 5.

32 Wiliam and Christodoulou, Assessment, Marking and Feedback, p. 27.

33 See Dylan Wiliam, Is the Feedback You're Giving Students Helping or Hindering?, *Dylan Wiliam Center* (29 November 2014). Available at: http://www.dylanwiliamcenter.com/is-the-feedback-you-are-giving-students-helping-or-hindering/.

Final Thoughts

This book has recommended a wide range of effective maths teaching strategies and, as such, aims to act as a catalyst for future thought and action. The strategies are yours to adapt and improve. Remember, only you are the expert in your classroom.

That said, "It's actually incredibly difficult to change our practice as teachers. It requires making a deliberate decision to make a change and then to persist with it until our default ideas and habits shift." Wise words from Tom Sherrington.[1] Reading books alone does not change our teaching. *Changing our teaching changes our teaching.*

Adding more and more strategies to your repertoire is likely to increase your workload. This is undesirable and unsustainable. For each change you make, try to drop something. Ask yourself, "What do I do that has the least impact?" Then stop doing it.

There are 52 strategies in this book – each one capable of nudging the impact of your teaching in the right direction. If you are unsure what to change first, start with these – my top picks for each of the six principles:

Chapter	Purpose	Strategy	
1	Challenge	1	Quantify and Ramp Up Challenge
2	Explanation and modelling	1	Isolate the Skill
		2	Worked Examples
3	Practice	7	Spaced Practice
4	Questioning	7	Hinge Questions
5	Feedback	1	Writing on Whiteboards

These and the other strategies in the book enable us to create more effective learning experiences for our students so they can experience greater success – especially since, as Dylan Wiliam puts it, "schooling is a one shot deal for our kids".[2]

Make every maths lesson count on a daily basis. Remember to share the love of your subject with your students. And, finally, remember that "if you try to catch five rabbits, you catch none".

Endnotes

1   Tom Sherrington, *The Learning Rainforest: Great Teaching in Real Classrooms* (Woodbridge: John Catt Educational, 2017), p. 17.

2   C. M. Rubin, The Global Search for Education: What Did You Learn Today? [interview with Dylan Wiliam], *Huffington Post* (20 September 2011).

Appendix
Index of Strategies

Bibliography

All Party Parliamentary Group for Maths and Numeracy (2014). Briefing Paper. Available at: http://www.nationalnumeracy.org.uk/sites/default/files/appg_briefing-paper.pdf.

Allen, Rebecca (2018). What If We Cannot Measure Pupil Progress?, *Musings on Education Policy* (23 May). Available at: https://rebeccaallen.co.uk/2018/05/23/what-if-we-cannot-measure-pupil-progress/.

Allen, Rebecca and Sam Sims (2018). *How Do Shortages of Maths Teachers Affect the Within-School Allocation of Maths Teachers to Pupils?* (London: Nuffield Foundation). Available at: http://www.nuffieldfoundation.org/sites/default/files/files/Within-school%20allocations%20of%20maths%20teachers%20to%20pupils_v_FINAL.pdf.

Allison, Shaun and Andy Tharby (2015). *Making Every Lesson Count: Six Principles to Support Great Teaching and Learning* (Carmarthen: Crown House Publishing).

Atkinson, Robert K., Alexander Renkl and Mary M. Merrill (2003). Transitioning from Studying Examples to Solving Problems: Effects of Self-Explanation Prompts and Fading Worked-Out Steps, *Journal of Educational Psychology* 95(4): 774–783. Available at: https://www.researchgate.net/publication/200772684_Transitioning_From_Studying_Examples_to_Solving_Problems_Effects_of_Self-Explanation_Prompts_and_Fading_Worked-Out_Steps.

Barbash, Shepard (2012). *Clear Teaching: With Direct Instruction* (Arlington, VA: Education Consumers Foundation).

Barton, Craig (2017a). Kris Boulton – Part 1: Planning Lessons, Engelmann and Differentiation, *Mr Barton Maths Podcast* [audio] (17 July). Available at: http://www.mrbartonmaths.com/blog/kris-boulton-part-1-planning-lessons-engelmann-and-differentiation/.

Barton, Craig (2017b). Doug Lemov: Teach Like a Champion and Top Tips for Delivering Training, *Mr Barton Maths Podcast* [audio] (13 November). Available at: http://www.mrbartonmaths.com/blog/doug-lemov-teach-like-a-champion-and-top-tips-for-delivering-training/.

Barton, Craig (2018a). *How I Wish I'd Taught Maths: Lessons Learned from Research, Conversations with Experts, and 12 Years of Mistakes* (Woodbridge: John Catt Educational).

Barton, Craig (2018b). Jane Jones: Ofsted, Observations, Marking, Reasoning, *Mr Barton Maths Podcast* [audio] (3 January). Available at: http://www.mrbartonmaths.com/blog/jane-jones-ofsted-observations-marking-reasoning/.

Bay-William, Jennifer M. and Amy Stokes-Levine (2017). The Role of Concepts and Procedures in Developing Fluency. In Denise Spangler and Jeffrey J. Wanko (eds), *Enhancing Professional Practice with Research Behind Principles to Action* (Reston: VA: NCTM), pp. 61–72.

Bennett, Tom (2018). Tom Bennett Speaks to Professor Daniel Willingham, *researchED* 1(1) (2018): 5–8. Available at: https://researched.org.uk/wp-content/uploads/delightful-downloads/2018/07/researchEDMagazine-June2018.pdf.

Boulton, Kris (2017a). Maths: Conceptual Understanding First, or Procedural Fluency?, *... To the Real* (11 June). Available at: https://tothereal.wordpress.com/2017/06/11/maths-conceptual-understanding-first-or-procedural-fluency/.

Boulton, Kris (2017b). My Best Planning – Part 1, … *To the Real* (12 August). Available at: https://tothereal.wordpress.com/2017/08/12/my-best-planning-part-1/.

Buxton, Laurie (1981). *Do You Panic About Maths? Coping with Maths Anxiety* (London: Heinemann Educational Books).

Carroll, John B. (1963). A Model for School Learning, *Teachers College Record* 64(8): 723–733.

Carroll, Lewis (1994 [1872]). *Through the Looking Glass* (London: Penguin).

Centre for Education Statistics and Evaluation (2018). *Cognitive Load Theory in Practice: Examples for the Classroom* (Sydney: CESE). Available at: https://www.cese.nsw.gov.au/images/stories/PDF/Cognitive_load_theory_practice_guide_AA.pdf.

Christodoulou, Daisy (2017). *Making Good Progress? The Future of Assessment for Learning* (Oxford: Oxford University Press).

Coe, Robert (2013). Improving Education: A Triumph of Hope Over Experience. Inaugural lecture, Durham University, 18 June. Available at: http://www.cem.org/attachments/publications/ImprovingEducation2013.pdf.

Coe, Robert, Cesare Aloisi, Steve Higgins and Lee Elliot Major (2014). *What Makes Great Teaching? Review of the Underpinning Research* (October) (London: Sutton Trust). Available at: https://www.suttontrust.com/wp-content/uploads/2014/10/What-Makes-Great-Teaching-REPORT.pdf.

Cook, Susan W., Ryan G. Duffy and Kimberly M. Fenn (2013). Consolidation and Transfer of Learning After Observing Hand Gesture, *Child Development* 84(6): 1863–1871. Available at: https://pdfs.semanticscholar.org/a606/ca16285d30ceb9aa6be15380efb0dcf0e7c6.pdf.

Crawford, Claire and Jonathan Cribb (2013). *Reading and Maths Skills at Age 10 and Earnings in Later Life: A Brief Analysis Using the British Cohort Study*. Research Report REP03 (London: Centre for Analysis of Youth Transitions). Available at: https://www.ifs.org.uk/caytpubs/CAYTreport03.pdf.

Deans for Impact (2015). *The Science of Learning* (Austin, TX: Deans for Impact). Available at: https://deansforimpact.org/wp-content/uploads/2016/12/The_Science_of_Learning.pdf.

Department for Education (2014). National Curriculum in England: Mathematics Programmes of Study. Statutory Guidance (July). Available at: https://www.gov.uk/government/publications/national-curriculum-in-england-mathematics-programmes-of-study/national-curriculum-in-england-mathematics-programmes-of-study.

Department for Education (2016). *Eliminating Unnecessary Workload Around Marking: Report of the Independent Teacher Workload Review Group* (March). Available at: https://www.gov.uk/government/publications/reducing-teacher-workload-marking-policy-review-group-report.

Department for Education (2018). Practical Tools: Example of a Feedback Policy (Secondary School) (July). Available at: https://www.gov.uk/government/publications/feedback-and-marking-reducing-teacher-workload.

Didau, David (2016). The Feedback Continuum: Why Reducing Feedback Helps Students Learn, *The Learning Spy* (1 November). Available at: https://learningspy.co.uk/learning/the-feedback-continuum/.

Dowker, Ann (2014). Intervention for Children with Mathematical Difficulties, *Better: Evidence-Based Education – Mathematics* 6(1): 10–11. Available at: http://www.betterevidence.org/issue-14/.

Drury, Helen (2018). *How to Teach Mathematics for Mastery* (Oxford: Oxford University Press).

Education Endowment Foundation (2018). Feedback: Teaching & Learning Toolkit (28 September). Available at: https://educationendowmentfoundation.org.uk/pdf/generate/?u=https://educationendowmentfoundation.org.uk/pdf/toolkit/?id=131&t=Teaching%20and%20Learning%20Toolkit&e=131&s=.

Emeny, William (2014a). Bar Modelling – A Powerful Visual Approach for Introducing Number Topics, *Great Maths Teaching Ideas* (26 December). Available at: http://www.greatmathsteachingideas.com/2014/12/26/bar-modelling-a-powerful-visual-approach-for-introducing-number-topics/.

Emeny, William (2014b). You've Never Seen the GCSE Maths Curriculum Like This Before ..., *Great Maths Teaching Ideas* (5 January). Available at: http://www.greatmathsteachingideas.com/2014/01/05/youve-never-seen-the-gcse-maths-curriculum-like-this-before/.

Emeny, William (2015). Algebra Tiles – From Counting to Completing the Square, *Great Maths Teaching Ideas* (4 April). Available at: http://www.greatmathsteachingideas.com/2015/04/04/algebra-tiles-from-counting-to-completing-the-square/.

Ericsson, K. Anders (2017). Deliberate Practice Is What I Preach, *TES* (31 March). Available at: https://www.tes.com/news/deliberate-practice-what-i-preach.

Ericsson, K. Anders, Ralf T. Krampe and Clemens Tesch-Roemer (1993). The Role of Deliberate Practice in the Acquisition of Expert Performance, *Psychological Review* 100(3): 363–406.

Fletcher-Wood, Harry (2018). What is Responsive Teaching?, *Improving Teaching* (3 June). Available at: https://improvingteaching.co.uk/2018/06/03/what-is-responsive-teaching/.

Fletcher-Wood, Harry, Ben Bignall, Lucy Blewett, Jen Calvert, Josh Goodrich and Emma McCrea (2018). *The Learning Curriculum* (London: Institute for Teaching). Available at: https://khsbpp.files.wordpress.com/2018/06/ift-learning-curriculum-v1-2.pdf.

Foster, Colin (n.d.). Sum Fractions, *Teach Secondary* 3(5): 48–49. Available at: http://www.foster77.co.uk/Foster,%20Teach%20Secondary,%20Sum%20fractions.pdf.

Foster, Colin (2017). *Questions Pupils Ask* (Leicester: Mathematical Association).

Friis, Deb and Emma McCrea (in press). *Deliberate Maths: Expertly Designed Practice Question Sets.*

Garon-Carrier, Gabrielle, Michel Boivin, Frédéric Guay, Yulia Kovas, Ginette Dionne, Jean-Pascal Lemelin, Jean R. Séguin, Frank Vitaro and Richard E. Tremblay (2016). Intrinsic Motivation and Achievement in Mathematics in Elementary School: A Longitudinal Investigation of Their Association, *Child Development* 87(1): 165–175. doi: 10.1111/cdev.12458

Gilbert, Gerard (2010). The Six Secrets of a Happy Classroom, *The Independent* (23 September). Available at: https://www.independent.co.uk/news/education/schools/the-six-secrets-of-a-happy-classroom-2086855.html.

Gilbert, Kelsey (2016). Self-Explanation as a Study Strategy for Math, *The Learning Scientists* (12 July). Available at: http://www.learningscientists.org/blog/2016/7/12-1.

Gonzalez, Jennifer (2017). Retrieval Practice: The Most Powerful Learning Strategy You're Not Using, *Cult of Pedagogy* (24 September). Available at: https://www.cultofpedagogy.com/retrieval-practice/.

Gladwell, Malcolm (2008). *Outliers: The Story of Success* (London: Penguin).

Griffin, Pete, Craig Jeavons, Jess Paul, Richard Perring and Nicola Bretscher (2017). *Teaching for Mastery: Questions, Tasks and Activities to Support Assessment in KS3* (Sheffield: National Centre for Excellence in the Teaching of Mathematics). Available at: https://www.ncetm.org.uk/files/66633120/secondary_assessment_materials_november_2017.pdf.

Griffin, Peter (1989). Teaching Takes Place in Time, Learning Takes Place Over Time, *Mathematics Teaching* 126: 12–13.

Hanushek, Eric (2004). What If There Are No 'Best Practices'?, *Scottish Journal of Political Economy* 51(2): 156–172.

Hattie, John (2008). *Visible Learning: A Synthesis of Over 800 Meta-Analyses Relating to Achievement* (Abingdon: Routledge).

Hattie, John (2012). Know Thy Impact, *Educational Leadership* 70(1): 18–23.

Hayward, Hugh, Emily Hunt and Anthony Lord (2014). *The Economic Value of Key Intermediate Qualifications: Estimating the Returns and Lifetime Productivity Gains to GCSEs, A Levels and Apprenticeships. Research Report* (London: Department for Education).

Henderson, Peter, Jeremy Hodgen, Colin Foster, Rachel Marks and Margaret Brown (2018). *Improving Mathematics in Key Stages Two and Three: Evidence Review* (London: Education Endowment Foundation). Available at: https://educationendowmentfoundation.org.uk/public/files/Publications/Campaigns/Maths/EEF_Maths_Evidence_Review.pdf.

Hodgen, Jeremy, Colin Foster and Dietmar Kuchemann (2018). *Improving Mathematics in Key Stages Two and Three: Guidance Report* (London: Education Endowment Foundation). Available at: https://educationendowmentfoundation.org.uk/tools/guidance-reports/maths-ks-two-three/.

Holt, John (1964). *How Children Fail* (London: Pitman).

Hughes, Elizabeth M., Sarah R. Powell and Elizabeth A. Stevens (2016). Supporting Clear and Concise Mathematical Language, *Teaching Exceptional Children* 49(1): 7–17.

Institute of Education Sciences (2015a). *Teaching Strategies for Improving Algebra Knowledge in Middle and High School Students* (Washington, DC: IES). Available at: https://ies.ed.gov/ncee/wwc/Docs/PracticeGuide/wwc_algebra_040715.pdf.

Institute of Education Sciences (2015b). Teaching Strategies for Improving Algebra Knowledge in Middle and High School Students: Practice Guide Summary. Available at: https://ies.ed.gov/ncee/wwc/Docs/practiceguide/wwc_algebra_summary_072115.pdf.

Karp, Karen S., Sarah B. Bush and Barbara J. Dougherty (2014). 13 Rules That Expire, *Teaching Children Mathematics* 21(1): 18–25.

Khan, Sal (2015). Let's Teach Mastery – Not Test Scores, *TED.com* [video]. Available at: https://www.ted.com/talks/sal_khan_let_s_teach_for_mastery_not_test_scores?language=en#t-279632.

Kaplinsky, Robert (2015). Depth of Knowledge Matrix – Elementary & Secondary Math, *Robert Kaplinsky* (4 February). Available at: https://robertkaplinsky.com/tool-to-distinguish-between-depth-of-knowledge-levels/.

Kaplinsky, Robert (2016). Shallowness (Not Depth) of Knowledge, *Robert Kaplinsky* (25 October). Available at: https://robertkaplinsky.com/shallowness-not-depth-knowledge/.

Kaplinsky, Robert (2017a). Depth of Knowledge Matrix – Elementary Math, *Robert Kaplinsky* (24 January). Available at: https://robertkaplinsky.com/depth-knowledge-matrix-elementary-math/.

Kaplinsky, Robert (2017b). Depth of Knowledge Matrix – Secondary Math, *Robert Kaplinsky* (31 January 2017). Available at: http://robertkaplinsky.com/depth-knowledge-matrix-secondary-math/.

Kirschner, Paul A., John Sweller and Richard E. Clark (2006). Why Minimal Guidance During Instruction Does Not Work: An Analysis of the Failure of Constructivist, Discovery, Problem-Based, Experiential, and Inquiry-Based Teaching, *Educational Psychologist* 41(2): 75–86.

Kluger, Avraham N. and Angelo S. DeNisi (1996). The Effects of Feedback Interventions on Performance: A Historical Review, a Meta-Analysis, and a Preliminary Feedback Intervention Theory, *Psychological Bulletin* 119(2): 254–284. Available at: https://www.researchgate.net/publication/232458848_The_Effects_of_Feedback_Interventions_on_Performance_A_Historical_Review_a_Meta-Analysis_and_a_Preliminary_Feedback_Intervention_Theory.

Kullberg, Angelika, Ulla Runesson Kempe and Ference Marton (2017). What Is Made Possible to Learn When Using the Variation Theory of Learning in Teaching Mathematics? *International Journal on Mathematics Education* 49: 559–569. Available at: https://link.springer.com/content/pdf/10.1007%2Fs11858-017-0858-4.pdf.

Lemov, Doug (2015). *Teach Like a Champion 2.0: 62 Techniques That Put Students on the Path to College* (San Francisco, CA: Jossey-Bass).

Lemov, Doug, Erica Woolway and Katie Yezzi (2012). *Practice Perfect: 42 Rules for Getting Better at Getting Better* (San Francisco, CA: Jossey-Bass).

McCourt, Mark (2018a). An Introduction to Algebra Tiles for Teaching Mathematics, *The Emaths Blog* (18 March). Available at: https://markmccourt.blogspot.com/2018/03/an-introduction-to-algebra-tiles-for.html.

McCourt, Mark (2018b). Teaching for Mastery – Part 3, *The Emaths Blog* (18 August). Available at: https://markmccourt.blogspot.com/2018/08/teaching-for-mastery-part-3_18.html.

Mccrea, Peps (2017). *Memorable Teaching: Leveraging Memory to Build Deep and Durable Learning in the Classroom* (n.p.: CreateSpace).

McGinn, Kelly M., Karin E. Lange and Julie L. Booth (2015). A Worked Example for Creating Worked Examples, *Mathematics Teaching in the Middle School* 21(1): 27–33. Available at: https://www.nctm.org/Publications/Mathematics-Teaching-in-Middle-School/2015/Vol21/Issue1/A-Worked-Example-for-Creating-Worked-Examples/.

Mason, John (2010). Effective Questioning and Responding in the Mathematics Classroom. Available at: https://www.researchgate.net/publication/234169730_Effective_Questioning_Responding.

Mattock, Peter (2018). *Visible Maths: Using Representations and Structure to Enhance Mathematics Teaching in Schools* (Carmarthen: Crown House Publishing).

Muijs, Daniel (2018). Making Evidence Count for the Busy Teacher. Presentation at researchEd, Durrington High School, Worthing, 28 April.

Murre, Jaap M. J. and Joeri Dros (2015). Replication and Analysis of Ebbinghaus' Forgetting Curve, *PLOS ONE* 10(7): e0120644. Available at: https://doi.org/10.1371/journal.pone.0120644.

National Academies of Sciences, Engineering, and Medicine (2018). *How People Learn II: Learners, Contexts, and Cultures* (Washington, DC: National Academies Press). Available at: https://doi.org/10.17226/24783.

National Association of Mathematics Advisers (2015). Five Myths of Mastery in Mathematics (December). Available at: http://www.nama.org.uk/Downloads/Five%20 Myths%20about%20Mathematics%20Mastery.pdf.

National Centre for Excellence in the Teaching of Mathematics (2008). *Mathematics Matters: Final Report* (Sheffield: NCETM). Available at: https://www.ncetm.org.uk/ public/files/309231/Mathematics+Matters+Final+Report.pdf.

National Centre for Excellence in the Teaching of Mathematics (2014). *Mathematics Glossary for Teachers in Key Stages 1 to 3* (January). Available at: https://www.ncetm.org. uk/files/19226855/National+Curriculum+Glossary.pdf.

National Centre for Excellence in the Teaching of Mathematics (2015). NCETM Mathematics Textbook Guidance (January). Available at: https://www.ncetm.org.uk/ files/21383193/NCETM+Textbook+Guidance.pdf.

National Centre for Excellence in the Teaching of Mathematics (2016). Guidance on Marking and Feedback for Secondary Mathematics Teaching (October). Available at: https://www.ncetm.org.uk/public/files/40764571/Secondary+Marking+Guidance+ (October+2016).pdf.

National Council of Teachers of Mathematics (2007). Five 'Key Strategies' for Effective Formative Assessment. Research Brief. Available at: https://www.nctm.org/ uploadedFiles/Research_and_Advocacy/research_brief_and_clips/Research_brief_04_-_ Five_Key%20Strategies.pdf.

National Numeracy (2015). *Attitudes Towards Maths: Research and Approach Overview.* (Lewes: National Numeracy). Available at: https://www.nationalnumeracy.org.uk/sites/ default/files/attitudes_towards_maths_-_updated_branding.pdf.

Newton, Elizabeth (1990). The Rocky Road from Actions to Intentions. Unpublished PhD dissertation, Stanford University.

Nuthall, Graham (2007). *The Hidden Lives of Learners* (Wellington: New Zealand Council for Educational Research).

Ofsted (2012). *Mathematics: Made to Measure* (May). Ref: 110159. Available at: https:// assets.publishing.service.gov.uk/government/uploads/system/uploads/attachment_data/ file/417446/Mathematics_made_to_measure.pdf.

Orlin, Ben (2016). What Students See When They Look at Algebra, *Man with Bad Drawings* (22 June). Available at: https://mathwithbaddrawings.com/2016/06/22/ what-students-see-when-they-look-at-algebra/.

Pashler, Harold, Patrice M. Bain, Brian A. Bottge, Arthur Graesser, Kenneth Koedinger, Mark McDaniel and Janet Metcalfe (2007). *Organizing Instruction and Study to Improve Student Learning: IES Practice Guide.* NCER 2007-2004 (Washington, DC: Institute of Education Sciences). Available at: https://ies.ed.gov/ncee/wwc/Docs/PracticeGuide/ 20072004.pdf.

Pershan, Michael (2016). Beyond 'Better-Luck-Next-Time' Feedback, *Heinemann Blog* (12 May). Available at: https://blog.heinemann.com/mpershan-feedbackupdate-5-12.

Pershan, Michael (2017). Feedbackless Feedback, *Teaching with Problems* (26 May). Available at: https://problemproblems.wordpress.com/2017/05/26/feedbackless- feedback/.

Petit, Marge and Karin Hess (2006). Applying Webb's Depth of Knowledge and NAEP Levels of Complexity in Mathematics. Available at: https://www.nciea.org/sites/ default/files/publications/DOKmath_KH08.pdf.

Picciotto, Henri (2018). More Catchphrases, *Henri's Math Education Blog* (8 November). Available at: https://blog.mathed.page/2018/11/08/more-catchphrases/.

Pro Bono Economics (2014). *Pro Bono Economics Report for National Numeracy: Cost of Outcomes Associated with Low Levels of Adult Numeracy in the UK*. Available at: https://www.probonoeconomics.com/sites/default/files/files/PBE%20National%20Numeracy%20costs%20report%2011Mar.pdf.

Quinn, Dani (2017). Never Let Me Go, *Until I Know Better* (31 May). Available at: https://missquinnmaths.wordpress.com/2017/05/31/never-let-me-go/.

Reddy, Bruno (2012). Guest Blog: Circle Theorems and Hula Hoops, *Mr Reddy Maths Blog* (10 December). Available at: http://mrreddy.com/blog/2012/12/guest-blog-circle-theorems-and-hula-hoops/.

Rittle-Johnson, Bethany and Nancy C. Jordan (2016). *Synthesis of IES-Funded Research on Mathematics: 2002–2013*. NCER 2016-2003 (Washington, DC: Institute of Education Sciences). Available at: https://ies.ed.gov/ncer/pubs/20162003/pdf/20162003.pdf.

Rittle-Johnson, Bethany, Michael Schneider and Jon R. Star (2015). Not a One-Way Street: Bidirectional Relations Between Procedural and Conceptual Knowledge of Mathematics, *Educational Psychology Review* 27(4): 587–597. DOI: 10.1007/s10648-015-9302-x

Rivers, Michelle (2018). How Test Expectancy Promotes Learning, *The Learning Scientists* (15 May). Available at: http://www.learningscientists.org/blog/2018/5/15-1.

Rizvi, Naveen (2018). Engelmann Insights: Structuring Teaching for the Weakest Pupils (Part 1), *Conception of the Good* (11 March). Available at: http://conceptionofthegood.co.uk/?p=569.

Roediger III, Henry L. and Jeffrey D. Karpicke (2006). Test-Enhanced Learning: Taking Memory Tests Improves Long-Term Retention, *Psychological Science* 17(3): 249–255. Available at: http://learninglab.psych.purdue.edu/downloads/2006_Roediger_Karpicke_PsychSci.pdf.

Rosenshine, Barak (2012). Principles of Instruction: Research-Based Strategies That All Teachers Should Know, *American Educator* (Spring): 12–39. Available at: https://www.aft.org/sites/default/files/periodicals/Rosenshine.pdf.

Rubin, C. M. (2011). The Global Search for Education: What Did You Learn Today? [interview with Dylan Wiliam], *Huffington Post* (20 September).

Rycroft-Smith, Lucy, Camilla Gilmore and Lucy Cragg (2017). Why Is Working Memory Important for Mathematics Learning?, *Espresso* 10. Available at: https://www.cambridgemaths.org/Images/429694-traditional-and-progressive.pdf.

Sherrington, Tom (2012). The Number 1 Bit of Classroom Kit: Mini-Whiteboards, *teacherhead* (28 August). Available at: https://teacherhead.com/2012/08/28/the-number-1-bit-of-classroom-kit-mini-whiteboards/.

Sherrington, Tom (2017). *The Learning Rainforest: Great Teaching in Real Classrooms* (Woodbridge: John Catt Educational).

Sherwood, Jemma (2018). *How to Enhance Your Mathematics Subject Knowledge: Number and Algebra for Secondary Teachers* (Oxford: Oxford University Press).

Shute, Valerie J. (2008). Focus on Formative Feedback, *Review of Educational Research* 78 (1): 153–189. Available at: https://www.researchgate.net/publication/220017728_Focus_on_Formative_Feedback.

Smith, Megan, Yana Weinstein and Oliver Caviglioli (2016). Concept Map: What Does Retrieval Practice Do?, *The Learning Scientists* (1 April). Available at: http://www.learningscientists.org/blog/2016/4/1-1.

Southall, Ed (2017). *Yes, But Why? Teaching for Understanding in Mathematics* (London: SAGE).

Stanovich, Keith E. (1986). Matthew Effects in Reading: Some Consequences of Individual Differences in the Acquisition of Literacy, *Reading Research Quarterly* 21(4): 360–407.

Steward, Don (2011). Circle Areas, *Median* (30 January). Available at: https://donsteward.blogspot.com/2011/01/circle-areas.html.

Sumeracki, Megan (2018). Retrieval Practice: Hiding Broccoli in the Brownies, *The Learning Scientists* (19 July). Available at: http://www.learningscientists.org/blog/2018/7/19-1.

Sutton Trust (2011). *Improving the Impact of Teachers on Pupil Achievement in the UK: Interim Findings* (September). Available at: https://www.suttontrust.com/wp-content/uploads/2011/09/2teachers-impact-report-final.pdf.

Swan, Malcolm (2005). *Standards Unit: Improving Learning in Mathematics: Challenges and Strategies* (London: Department for Education and Skills). Available at: https://www.ncetm.org.uk/public/files/224/improving_learning_in_mathematicsi.pdf.

Swan, Malcolm (2006). *Collaborative Learning in Mathematics: A Challenge to Our Beliefs and Practices* (London: National Research and Development Centre/National Institute of Adult Continuing Education).

Sweller, John (2016). Story of a Research Program. In Sigmund Tobias, Dexter Fletcher and David Berliner (series eds), Acquired Wisdom Series. *Education Review* 23. Available at: http://dx.doi.org/10.14507/er.v23.2025.

Sweller, John, Paul Ayres and Slava Kalyuga (2011). *Cognitive Load Theory* (New York: Springer).

Tharby, Andy (2017). Content, Thinking and Shaping: Three Principles for Working with Brighter Students, *Reflecting English* (30 January). Available at: https://reflectingenglish.wordpress.com/2017/01/30/content-thinking-and-shaping-three-principles-for-working-with-brighter-students/.

Tharby, Andy (2018). What Does Research Evidence Tell Us About Effective Questioning? *Research Schools Network* (24 May). Available at: https://durrington.researchschool.org.uk/2018/05/24/what-does-research-evidence-tell-us-about-effective-questioning/.

Wakefield, Elizabeth, Miriam A. Novack, Eliza L. Congdon, Steven Franconeri and Susan Goldin-Meadow (2018). Gesture Helps Learners Learn, But Not Merely By Guiding Their Visual Attention, *Developmental Science* 21(6): e12664. Available at: http://visualthinking.psych.northwestern.edu/publications/WakefieldGesture2018.pdf.

Watson, Anne (ed.) (2018). *Variation in Mathematics Teaching and Learning. A Collection of Writing from ATM: Mathematics Teaching* (Derby: Association of Teachers of Mathematics).

Watson, Anne and John Mason (1998). *Questions and Prompts for Mathematical Thinking* (Derby: Association of Teachers of Mathematics).

Watson, Anne and John Mason (2006). Seeing an Exercise As a Single Mathematical Object: Using Variation to Structure Sense-Making, *Mathematics Thinking and Learning*

8(2): 91–111. Available at: http://oro.open.ac.uk/9764/1/06_MTL_Watson_%26_ Mason.pdf.

Weinstein, Yana and Megan Sumeracki (2019). *Understanding How We Learn: A Visual Guide* (Abingdon and New York: Routledge).

Wiliam, Dylan (2006). Assessment for Learning: Why, What and How? Edited transcript of a talk given at the Cambridge Assessment Network Conference at the Faculty of Education, University of Cambridge, 15 September. Available at: http:// www.dylanwiliam.org/Dylan_Wiliams_website/Papers.html.

Wiliam, Dylan (2007). Content *Then* Process: Teacher Learning Communities in the Service of Formative Assessment. In Douglas B. Reeves (ed.), *Ahead of the Curve: The Power of Assessment to Transform Teaching and Learning* (Bloomington, IN: Solution Tree Press), pp. 183–206.

Wiliam, Dylan (2011). *Embedded Formative Assessment* (Bloomington, IN: Solution Tree Press).

Wiliam, Dylan (2014a). Is the Feedback You're Giving Students Helping or Hindering?, *Dylan Wiliam Center* (29 November). Available at: http://www.dylanwiliamcenter.com/ is-the-feedback-you-are-giving-students-helping-or-hindering/.

Wiliam, Dylan (2014b). Why Teaching Will Never Be a Research-Based Profession and Why That's a Good Thing. Presentation at researchED, Harris Academy, London, 8 September.

Wiliam, Dylan and Daisy Christodoulou (2017). Assessment, Marking and Feedback. In Carl Hendrick and Robin Macpherson (eds), *What Does This Look Like in the Classroom?* (Woodbridge: John Catt Educational), pp. 22–44.

Willingham, Daniel T. (2009) Why Don't Students Like School? Because the Mind Is Not Designed for Thinking, *American Educator* (Spring): 4–13. Available at: https://www. aft.org/sites/default/files/periodicals/WILLINGHAM%282%29.pdf.

Willingham, Daniel T. (2009–2010). Is It True That Some People Just Can't Do Math?, *American Educator* (Winter): 14–19, 39. Available at: https://www.aft.org/sites/default/ files/periodicals/willingham.pdf.

Willingham, Daniel T. (2010). *Why Don't Students Like School? A Cognitive Scientist Answers Questions About How the Mind Works and What It Means for the Classroom* (San Francisco, CA: Jossey-Bass).

Willingham, Daniel T. (2017). Do Manipulatives Help Students Learn?, *American Educator* (Fall): 25–40. Available at: https://www.aft.org/sites/default/files/periodicals/ ae_fall2017_willingham.pdf.

Woodward, John, Sybilla Beckmann, Mark Driscoll, Megan Franke, Patricia Herzig, Asha Jitendra, Kenneth R. Koedinger and Philip Ogbuehi (2012). *Improving Mathematical Problem Solving in Grades 4 Through 8*. IES Practice Guide. NCEE 2012-4055 (Washington, DC: Institute of Education Sciences).

Wragg, Edward and George Brown (2001). *Questioning in the Secondary School* (Abingdon: Routledge).

Permissions

Extract on page 15: © Daniel T. Willingham, Is It True That Some People Just Can't Do Math?, *American Educator* (Winter 2009–2010): 14–19, 39 at 16. Available at: https://www.aft.org/sites/default/files/periodicals/willingham.pdf. Used with kind permission.

Figure 1.1: © Robert Coe, Improving Education: A Triumph of Hope Over Experience. Inaugural lecture, Durham University, 18 June 2013. Available at: http://www.cem.org/attachments/publications/ImprovingEducation2013.pdf, p. xii. Used with kind permission.

John Mason's circle areas problem, featured in Figure 1.4: This problem can be seen at Don Steward, Circle Areas, *Median* (30 January 2011). Available at: https://donsteward.blogspot.com/2011/01/circle-areas.html. © John Mason and reproduced with kind permission.

Figure 1.5: © Robert Kaplinsky, Shallowness (Not Depth) of Knowledge, *Robert Kaplinsky* (25 October 2016). Available at: https://robertkaplinsky.com/shallowness-not-depth-knowledge/. Used with kind permission.

Table 1.1: © Marge Petit and Karin Hess, Applying Webb's Depth of Knowledge and NAEP Levels of Complexity in Mathematics (2006). Available at: https://www.nciea.org/sites/default/files/publications/DOKmath_KH08.pdf, p. 1.

Figure 1.6: Adapted from the original © Robert Kaplinsky, Depth of Knowledge Matrix – Secondary Math, *Robert Kaplinsky* (31 January 2017). Available at: http://robertkaplinsky.com/depth-knowledge-matrix-secondary-math/; and Robert Kaplinsky, Depth of Knowledge Matrix – Elementary & Secondary Math, *Robert Kaplinsky* (4 February 2015). Used with kind permission.

Figure 1.7: © Robert Kaplinsky and Nanette Johnson via http://www.openmiddle.com. Used with kind permission.

Figure 1.9: © Colin Foster, Sum Fractions, *Teach Secondary* 3(5): 48–49. Available at: http://www.foster77.co.uk/Foster,%20Teach%20Secondary,%20Sum%20fractions.pdf. Used with author's kind permission.

Figure 1.11: © Marcus Bennison, created as part of his subject knowledge enhancement course.

Table 2.1: Adapted from the original © Elizabeth M. Hughes, Sarah R. Powell and Elizabeth A. Stevens, Supporting Clear and Concise Mathematical Language, *Teaching Exceptional Children* 49(1) (2016): 7–17; Institute of Education Sciences, *Teaching Strategies for Improving Algebra Knowledge in Middle and High School Students* (Washington, DC: IES, 2015). Available at: https://ies.ed.gov/ncee/wwc/Docs/PracticeGuide/wwc_algebra_040715.pdf (used with authors' kind permission); and Karen S. Karp, Sarah B. Bush and Barbara J. Dougherty, 13 Rules That Expire, *Teaching Children Mathematics* 21(1) (2014): 18–25.

Figures 2.4, 2.5 and 2.22: Excerpts from AlgebraByExample used with permission of SERP @ Strategic Education Research Partnership serpinstitute.org.

Figure 3.3: Adapted from the original © Peps Mccrea, *Memorable Teaching: Leveraging Memory to Build Deep and Durable Learning in the Classroom* (n.p.: CreateSpace), p. 14. Used with kind permission.

Figures 3.4 and 3.5: © Anne Watson and John Mason (2006). Seeing an Exercise As a Single Mathematical Object: Using Variation to Structure Sense-Making, *Mathematics*

Making Every Science Lesson Count

Six principles to support great science teaching

Shaun Allison

ISBN: 978-178583182-9

Making Every Science Lesson Count goes in search of answers to the fundamental question that all science teachers must ask: "What can I do to help my students become the scientists of the future?"

Shaun points a sceptical finger at the fashions and myths that have pervaded science teaching over the past decade or so and presents a range of tools and techniques that will help science teachers make abstract ideas more concrete and practical demonstrations more meaningful.

Making Every English Lesson Count

Six principles to support great reading and writing

Andy Tharby

ISBN: 978-178583179-9

Brings the teaching of conceptual knowledge, vocabulary and challenging literature to the foreground and shows teachers how to develop students' reading and writing proficiency over time.

Andy taps into the transformational effect that quality English teaching can have, and talks secondary school English teachers through effective methods that will challenge students to read and think beyond the confines of their world.

Making Every Geography Lesson Count

Six principles to support
great geography teaching

Mark Enser

ISBN: 978-178583339-7

Maps out the key elements of effective geography teaching to help teachers ensure that their students leave their lessons with an improved knowledge of the world, a better understanding of how it works and the geographical skills to support their understanding.

Mark offers an inspiring alternative to restrictive Ofsted-driven definitions of great teaching, and empowers geography teachers to deliver great lessons and celebrate high-quality practice.

Making Every MFL Lesson Count

Six principles to support great foreign language teaching

James A. Maxwell

ISBN: 978-178583396-0

Making Every MFL Lesson Count equips modern foreign language (MFL) teachers with practical techniques designed to enhance their students' linguistic awareness and to help them transfer the target language into long-term memory.

Written for new and experienced practitioners alike, *Making Every MFL Lesson Count* skilfully marries evidence-based practice with collective experience and, in doing so, inspires a challenging approach to secondary school MFL teaching.

Making Every History Lesson Count

Six principles to support
great history teaching

Chris Runeckles

ISBN: 978-178583336-6

Writing in the practical, engaging style of the award-winning *Making Every Lesson Count*, Chris Runeckles articulates the fundamentals of great history teaching and shares simple, realistic strategies designed to deliver memorable lessons.

The book equips history teachers with the tools and techniques to help students better engage with the subject matter and develop more sophisticated historical analysis and arguments.

Making Every Lesson Count

Six principles to support great teaching and learning

Shaun Allison and Andy Tharby

ISBN: 978-184590973-4

This award-winning title has now inspired a whole series of books. Each of the books in the series are held together by six pedagogical principles – challenge, explanation, modelling, practice, feedback and questioning – and provide simple, realistic strategies that teachers can use to develop the teaching and learning in their classrooms.

A toolkit of techniques that teachers can use every lesson to make that lesson count. No gimmicky teaching – just high-impact and focused teaching that results in great learning, every lesson, every day.

Suitable for all teachers – including trainee teachers, NQTs and experienced teachers – who want quick and easy ways to enhance their practice.

ERA Educational Book Award winner 2016. Judges' comments: "A highly practical and interesting resource with loads of information and uses to support and inspire teachers of all levels of experience. An essential staffroom book."